CORPORATE FINANCE WORKBOOK

CFA Institute is the premier association for investment professionals around the world, with more than 150,000 CFA charterholders worldwide in 165+ countries and regions. Since 1963 the organization has developed and administered the renowned Chartered Financial Analyst® Program. With a rich history of leading the investment profession, CFA Institute has set the highest standards in ethics, education, and professional excellence within the global investment community and is the foremost authority on investment profession conduct and practice. Each book in the CFA Institute Investment Series is geared toward industry practitioners along with graduate-level finance students and covers the most important topics in the industry. The authors of these cutting-edge books are themselves industry professionals and academics and bring their wealth of knowledge and expertise to this series.

CORPORATE FINANCE WORKBOOK

Economic Foundations and Financial Modeling

Third Edition

Michelle R. Clayman, CFA

Martin S. Fridson, CFA

George H. Troughton, CFA

WILEY

Published by John Wiley & Sons, Inc., Hoboken, New Jersey
Published simultaneously in Canada

For general information on our other products and services or for technical support, please contact our Customer Care Department within the United States at (800) 762-2974, outside the United States at (317) 572-3993 or fax (317) 572-4002.

Wiley also publishes its books in a variety of electronic formats. Some content that appears in print may not be available in electronic formats. For more information about Wiley products, visit our web site at www.wiley.com.

ISBN 978-1-119-74381-1 (paper); ISBN 978-1-119-74379-8 (ebk);
ISBN 978-1-119-74383-5 (ebk)

Printed in the United States of America

SKY10036083_091522

CONTENTS

PART I

LEARNING OUTCOMES, SUMMARY, AND PRACTICE PROBLEMS

CHAPTER 1

CORPORATE STRUCTURES AND OWNERSHIP

LEARNING OUTCOMES

The candidate should be able to:

- compare business structures and describe key features of corporate issuers
- compare public and private companies
- compare the financial claims and motivations of lenders and owners

SUMMARY

- Common forms of business structures include sole proprietorships, general and limited partnerships, and corporations.
- Sole proprietorships and partnerships are considered extensions of their owner or partner(s). This largely means that profits are taxed at the individual's personal rates and individuals are fully liable for all of the business's debts.
- Limited partnerships and corporations allow for the specialization of expertise in operator roles, in addition to the re-distribution of risk and return sharing between owners, partners, and operators.
- The corporate form of business structure is preferred when capital requirements are greater than what could be raised through other business structures.
- A corporation is a legal entity separate and distinct from its owners. Owners have limited liability, meaning that only their investment is at risk of loss.
- Corporations raise capital by selling an ownership interest and by borrowing money. They issue stocks, or shares, to equity investors who are owners. Debt represents money borrowed from lenders. Long-term lenders are issued bonds.
- Nonprofit corporations are formed to promote a public benefit, religious benefit, or charitable mission. They do not have shareholders, they do not distribute dividends, and they generally do not pay taxes.
- For-profit corporations can be public or private.
- In many jurisdictions, corporate profits are taxed twice: once at the corporate level and again at the individual level when profits are distributed as dividends to the owners.
- Public corporations are usually listed on an exchange and ownership is easily transferable.

- Private corporations are not listed on an exchange and, therefore, have no observable stock price, making their valuation more challenging. Transactions between buyers and sellers are negotiated privately, and ownership transfer is much more difficult.
- The market capitalization of a public company is equal to share price multiplied by number of shares outstanding.
- Enterprise value represents the total value of the company and is equal to the sum of the market capitalization and the market value of net debt. (Net debt is debt less cash.)
- Public companies are subject to greater regulatory and disclosure requirements—most notably, the public disclosure of financial information through periodic filings with their regulator. Private companies are not required to make such disclosures to the public.
- Given greater risks, only accredited investors are permitted to invest in private companies.
- Corporations have a life cycle with four distinct stages: start-up, growth, maturity, and decline.
- Although corporations begin as private companies, many eventually choose to go public or are acquired by public companies. IPOs typically occur in the growth phase and are usually driven by capital needs to fund growth.
- In many developed countries, it has become easier for private companies to access the capital they need without having to go public. As a result, the number of listed (public) companies in developed countries has been trending downwards. The number of listed companies in emerging economies continues to grow.
- Debt (bonds) represents a contractual obligation on the part of the issuing company. The corporation is obligated to make the promised interest payments to the debtholders and to return the principal. Equity (stocks) does not involve a contractual obligation.
- Interest payments on debt are typically a tax-deductible expense for the corporation. Dividend payments on equity are not tax deductible.
- Debtholders have claim priority, but they are entitled only to the interest payments and the return of principal. Equityholders have no priority in claims.
- Therefore, from the investor's perspective, investing in equity is riskier than investing in debt. Equityholders do have a residual claim, meaning that they are entitled to whatever firm value remains after paying off the priority claim holders, which grants them unlimited upside potential.
- From the corporation's perspective, issuing debt is riskier than issuing equity. A corporation that cannot meet its contractual obligations to the debtholders can be forced into bankruptcy and liquidation.
- Potential conflicts can occur between debtholders and equityholders. Debtholders would prefer the corporation to invest in safer projects that produce smaller, more certain cash flows that are large enough to service the debt. Equityholders would prefer riskier projects that have much larger return potential, which they do not share with the debtholders.

PRACTICE PROBLEMS

1. Describe the process of going public by a private company.

2. Describe the process of going private by a public company.

3. Identify the true statement(s) about corporation types from among the following:
   A. Nonprofit corporations by definition cannot generate profits.
   B. Transferring ownership from seller to buyer is more difficult for a private company than for a public company.
   C. Companies are categorized as public when they have greater than a minimum number of shareholders.

4. From the corporate issuer's perspective, the risk level of bonds compared to stocks is _____.
   A. lower
   B. higher
   C. the same

5. True or false: Bondholders can become shareholders through non-market-based means. Justify your answer.
   A. True.
   B. False.

6. Explain potential conflicts of interest between debtholders and equityholders.

7. State a reason for the declining number of public companies in developed markets.

CHAPTER 2

INTRODUCTION TO CORPORATE GOVERNANCE AND OTHER ESG CONSIDERATIONS

LEARNING OUTCOMES

The candidate should be able to:

- describe a company's stakeholder groups and compare their interests
- describe the principal-agent relationship and conflicts that may arise between stakeholder groups
- describe corporate governance and mechanisms to manage stakeholder relationships and mitigate associated risks
- describe both the potential risks of poor corporate governance and stakeholder management and the benefits from effective corporate governance and stakeholder management
- describe environmental, social, and governance considerations in investment analysis
- describe environmental, social, and governance investment approaches

SUMMARY

The investment community is increasingly recognizing and quantifying environmental and social considerations and the impacts of corporate governance in the investment process. Analysts who understand these considerations can better evaluate their associated implications and risks for an investment decision. The core concepts covered are listed here:

- The primary stakeholder groups of a corporation consist of shareholders, creditors, the board of directors, managers and employees, customers, suppliers, and government/regulators.
- A principal-agent relationship (or agency relationship) entails a principal hiring an agent to perform a particular task or service. In a company, both the board of directors and management act in agent capacity to represent the interests of shareholder principals.

- Conflicts occur when the interests of various stakeholder groups diverge and when the interests of one group are compromised for the benefit of another.
- Stakeholder management involves identifying, prioritizing, and understanding the interests of stakeholder groups and managing the company's relationships with stakeholders.
- Mechanisms to mitigate shareholder risks include company reporting and transparency, general meetings, investor activism, derivative lawsuits, and corporate takeovers.
- Mechanisms to mitigate creditor risks include bond indenture(s), company reporting and transparency, and committee participation.
- Mechanisms to mitigate board risks include board/management meetings and board committees.
- Remaining mechanisms to mitigate risks for other stakeholders (employees, customers, suppliers, and regulators) include policies, laws, regulations, and codes.
- Executive (internal) directors are employed by the company and are typically members of senior management. Non-executive (external) directors have limited involvement in daily operations but serve an important oversight role.
- Two primary duties of a board of directors are duty of care and duty of loyalty.
- A company's board of directors typically has several committees that are responsible for specific functions and report to the board. Although the types of committees may vary across organization, the most common are the audit committee, governance committee, remuneration (compensation) committee, nomination committee, risk committee, and investment committee.
- Shareholder activism encompasses a range of strategies that may be used by shareholders when seeking to compel a company to act in a desired manner.
- From a corporation's perspective, risks of poor governance include weak control systems; ineffective decision making; and legal, regulatory, reputational, and default risk. Benefits include better operational efficiency, control, and operating and financial performance, as well as lower default risk (or cost of debt), which enhances shareholder value.
- Key analyst considerations in corporate governance and stakeholder management include economic ownership and voting control, board of directors' representation, remuneration and company performance, investor composition, strength of shareholders' rights, and the management of long-term risks.
- Environmental and social issues, such as climate change, air pollution, and societal impacts of a company's products and services, have historically been treated as negative externalities. However, increased stakeholder awareness and strengthening regulations are internalizing environmental and societal costs into the company's income statement by responsible investors.
- ESG investment approaches are *value*-based or *values*-based. There are six common ESG investment approaches: negative screening, positive screening, ESG integration, thematic investing, engagement/active ownership, and impact investing.

PRACTICE PROBLEMS

1. Which group of company stakeholders would be *least* affected if the firm's financial position weakens?
    A. Suppliers
    B. Customers
    C. Managers and employees

2. Which of the following represents a principal-agent conflict between shareholders and management?
    A. Risk tolerance
    B. Multiple share classes
    C. Accounting and reporting practices

3. Which of the following statements regarding stakeholder management is *most* accurate?
    A. Company management ensures compliance with all applicable laws and regulations.
    B. Directors are excluded from voting on transactions in which they hold material interest.
    C. The use of variable incentive plans in executive remuneration is decreasing.

4. Which of the following issues discussed at a shareholders' general meeting would *most likely* require only a simple majority vote for approval?
    A. Voting on a merger
    B. Election of directors
    C. Amendments to bylaws

5. Which of the following statements about environmental, social, and governance (ESG) in investment analysis is correct?
    A. ESG factors are strictly intangible in nature.
    B. ESG terminology is easily distinguishable among investors.
    C. Environmental and social factors have been adopted in investment analysis more slowly than governance factors.

6. The existence of "stranded assets" is a specific concern among investors of:
    A. energy companies.
    B. health care companies.
    C. property companies.

7. An investor concerned about clean-up costs resulting from breaches in a publicly traded company's safety standards would *most likely* consider which factors in her investment analysis?
    A. Social factors
    B. Governance factors
    C. Environmental factors

8. _____ investing is the umbrella term used to describe investment strategies that incorporate environmental, social, and governance (ESG) factors into their approaches.
    A. ESG
    B. Sustainable
    C. Responsible

9. An investor concerned about a publicly traded company's data privacy and security practices would *most likely* incorporate which type of ESG factors in an investment analysis?
   A. Social
   B. Governance
   C. Environmental

10. Which of the following statements regarding ESG investment approaches is *most accurate*?
    A. Negative screening excludes industries and companies that do not meet the investor's ESG criteria.
    B. Thematic investing considers multiple factors.
    C. Positive screening excludes industries with unfavorable ESG aspects.

11. Which of the following stakeholders are *least likely* to be positively affected by increasing the proportion of debt in the capital structure?
    A. Senior management
    B. Non-management employees
    C. Shareholders

12. Which statement correctly describes corporate governance?
    A. Corporate governance complies with a set of global standards.
    B. Corporate governance is independent of both shareholder theory and stakeholder theory.
    C. Corporate governance seeks to minimize and manage conflicting interests between insiders and external shareholders.

13. Which of the following represents a responsibility of a company's board of directors?
    A. Implementation of strategy
    B. Enterprise risk management
    C. Considering the interests of shareholders only

14. Which of the following statements concerning the legal environment and shareholder protection is *most* accurate?
    A. A civil law system offers better protection of shareholder interests than does a common law system.
    B. A common law system offers better protection of shareholder interests than does a civil law system.
    C. Neither system offers an advantage over the other in the protection of shareholder interests.

CHAPTER 3

WORKING CAPITAL & LIQUIDITY

LEARNING OUTCOMES

The candidate should be able to:

- compare methods to finance working capital
- explain expected relations between working capital, liquidity, and short-term funding needs (NEW)
- describe sources of primary and secondary liquidity and factors affecting a company's liquidity position
- compare a company's liquidity position with that of peers
- evaluate short-term funding choices available to a company

SUMMARY

Here we considered key aspects of short-term financial management: the choices available to fund a company's working capital needs and effective liquidity management. Both are critical in ensuring a company's day-to-day operations and ability to remain in business.

Key points of coverage included the following:

- Internal and external sources available to finance working capital needs and considerations in their selection
- Working capital approaches, their considerations, and their impact on the funding needs of the company
- Primary and secondary sources of liquidity and factors that can enhance a company's liquidity position
- The evaluation of a company's liquidity position and comparison to peers
- The evaluation of short-term financing choices based on their characteristics and effective costs

PRACTICE PROBLEMS

1. Two analysts are discussing the costs of external financing sources. The first states that the company's bonds have a known interest rate but that the interest rate on accounts

payable and the interest rate on equity financing are not specified. They are implicitly zero. Upon hearing this, the second analyst advocates financing the firm with greater amounts of accounts payable and common shareholders equity. Is the second analyst correct in his analysis?

A. He is correct in his analysis of accounts payable only.

B. He is correct in his analysis of common equity financing only.

C. He is not correct in his analysis of either accounts payable or equity financing.

2. A company has arranged a $20 million line of credit with a bank, allowing the company the flexibility to borrow and repay any amount of funds as long as the balance does not exceed the line of credit. These arrangements are called:

A. convertibles.

B. factoring.

C. revolvers.

3. The SOA Company needs to raise 75 million, in local currency, for substantial new investments next year. Specific details, all in local currency, are as follows:

- Investments of 10 million in receivables and 15 million in inventory will be made. Fixed capital investments of 50 million, including 10 million to replace depreciated equipment and 40 million of net new investments, will also be made.
- Net income is expected to be 30 million, and dividend payments will be 12 million. Depreciation charges will be 10 million.
- Short-term financing from accounts payable of 6 million is expected. The firm will use receivables as collateral for an 8 million loan. The firm will also issue a 14 million short-term note to a commercial bank.
- Any additional external financing needed can be raised from an increase in long-term bonds. If additional financing is not needed, any excess funds will be used to repurchase common shares.

What additional financing does SOA require?

A. SOA will need to issue 19 million of bonds.

B. SOA will need to issue 26 million of bonds.

C. SOA can repurchase 2 million of common shares.

4. XY1 Corporation's CFO has decided to pursue a moderate approach to funding the firm's working capital. Which of the following methods would best fit that particular approach?

A. Finance permanent and variable current assets with long-term financing.

B. Finance permanent and variable current assets with short-term financing.

C. Finance permanent current assets with long-term financing and variable current assets with short-term financing.

5. Kwam Solutions must raise €120 million. Kwam has two primary sources of liquidity: €60 million of marketable securities (which can be sold with minimal liquidation/ brokerage costs) and €30 million of bonds (which can be sold with 3% liquidation costs). Kwam can sell some or all of either of these portfolios. Kwam has a secondary source of liquidity, which would be to sell a large piece of real estate valued at €70 million (which would incur 10% liquidation costs). If Kwam sells the real estate, it must be sold entirely. (A fractional sale is not possible.) What is the lowest cost strategy for raising the needed €120 million?

A. Sell €60 million of the marketable securities, €30 million of the bonds, and €34.3 million of the real estate property.

B. Sell the real estate property and €50 million of the marketable securities.

C. Sell the real estate property and €57 million of the marketable securities.

6. A company increasing its credit terms for customers from 1/10, net 30 to 1/10, net 60 will *most likely* experience:
   A. an increase in cash on hand.
   B. a lower level of uncollectible accounts.
   C. an increase in the average collection period.

7. Paloma Villarreal has received three suggestions from her staff about how to address her firm's liquidity problems.

   Suggestion 1. Reduce the firm's inventory turnover rate.

   Suggestion 2. Reduce the average collection period on accounts receivable.

   Suggestion 3. Accelerate the payments on accounts payable by paying invoices before their due dates.

   Which suggestion should Villarreal employ to improve the firm's liquidity position?
   A. Suggestion 1
   B. Suggestion 2
   C. Suggestion 3

8. Selected liquidity ratios for three firms in the leisure products industry are given in the table below. The most recent fiscal year ratio is shown along with the average of the previous five years.

	Company H		Company J		Company S	
	Most Recent	Five-Year Average	Most Recent	Five-Year Average	Most Recent	Five-Year Aaverage
Current ratio	5.37	2.51	3.67	3.04	3.05	2.53
Quick ratio	5.01	2.19	2.60	2.01	1.78	1.44
Cash ratio	3.66	0.97	1.96	1.28	0.96	0.67

   Relative to its peers and relative to its own prior performance, which company is in the most liquid position?
   A. Company H
   B. Company J
   C. Company S

9. An analyst is examining the cash conversion cycles and their components for three companies that she covers in the leisure products industry. She believes that changes in the investments in these working capital accounts can reveal liquidity stresses on a company.

	2021	2020	2019	2018	2017	2016
Company H						
Days of inventory on hand	68.4	70.5	60	57.8	59.8	59.8
+ Days of receivables	101.8	103.4	95.6	92.4	94.7	93.3
– Days of payables outstanding	52.1	54.6	48	41.9	36.8	35.9
= Cash conversion cycle	118.1	119.3	107.6	108.3	117.7	117.2
Company J						
Days of inventory on hand	105.6	101.4	96.3	105.2	103.2	101.4
+ Days of receivables	27.7	29.4	32.9	36.3	37.8	38
– Days of payables outstanding	36.6	38.5	35.3	39.3	37.8	40.2
= Cash conversion cycle	96.7	92.3	93.9	102.2	103.2	99.2
Company S						
Days of inventory on hand	135.8	131	118.9	69.2	63.4	81.7
+ Days of receivables	49.1	42.5	54.2	36.2	29.1	38.3
– Days of payables outstanding	30.9	27.9	34.6	29.8	31.8	35.9
= Cash conversion cycle	154.0	145.6	138.5	75.6	60.7	84.1

Which company's operating cycle appears to have caused the most liquidity stress?
A. Company H's
B. Company J's
C. Company S's

10. Which of the following are considered internal sources of financing for a company's working capital management?
    A. Committed and uncommitted lines of credit
    B. Accounts receivable and inventory
    C. Accounts payable and accruals

CHAPTER 4

CAPITAL INVESTMENTS

LEARNING OUTCOMES

The candidate should be able to:

- describe types of capital investments made by companies
- describe the capital allocation process and basic principles of capital allocation
- demonstrate the use of net present value (NPV) and internal rate of return (IRR) in allocating capital and describe the advantages and disadvantages of each method
- describe common capital allocation pitfalls
- describe expected relations among a company's investments, company value, and share price
- describe types of real options relevant to capital investment

SUMMARY

Capital investments—those investments with a life of one year or longer—are key in determining whether a company is profitable and generating value for its shareholders. Capital allocation is the process companies use to decide their capital investment activity. This chapter introduces capital investments, basic principles underlying the capital allocation model, and the use of NPV and IRR decision criteria.

- Companies invest for two reasons: to maintain their existing businesses and to grow them. Projects undertaken by companies to maintain a business including operating efficiencies are (1) going concern projects and (2) regulatory/compliance projects, while (3) expansion projects and (4) other projects are undertaken by companies to strategically expand or grow their operations.
- Capital allocation supports the most critical investments for many corporations—their investments in long-term assets. The principles of capital allocation are also relevant and can be applied to other corporate investing and financing decisions and to security analysis and portfolio management.
- The typical steps companies take in the capital allocation process are (1) idea generation, (2) investment analysis, (3) capital allocation planning, and (4) post-audit/monitoring.
- Companies should base their capital allocation decisions on the investment project's incremental after-tax cash flows discounted at the opportunity cost of funds. In addition,

companies should ignore financing costs because both the cost of debt and the cost of other capital are captured in the discount rate used in the analysis.

- The NPV of an investment project is the present value of its after-tax cash flows (or the present value of its after-tax cash inflows minus the present value of its after-tax outflows) or

$$NPV = \sum_{t=0}^{n} \frac{CF_t}{(1+r)^t},$$

where the investment outlays are negative cash flows included in CF_t and r is the required rate of return for the investment.

- Microsoft Excel functions to solve for the NPV for both conventional and unconventional cash flow patterns are

  - NPV or =NPV(rate, values) and
  - XNPV or =XNPV(rate, values, dates),

  where "rate" is the discount rate, "values" are the cash flows, and "dates" are the dates of each of the cash flows.

- The IRR is the discount rate that makes the present value of all future cash flows of the project sum to zero. This equation can be solved for the IRR:

$$\sum_{t=0}^{n} \frac{CF_t}{(1+IRR)^t} = 0.$$

- Using Microsoft Excel functions to solve for IRR, the functions are

  - IRR or =IRR(values, guess) and
  - XIRR or =XIRR(values, dates, guess),

  where "values" are the cash flows, "guess" is an optional user-specified guess that defaults to 10%, and "dates" are the dates of each cash flow.

- Companies should invest in a project if the NPV > 0 or if the IRR > r.
- For mutually exclusive investments that are ranked differently by the NPV and IRR, the NPV criterion is the more economically sound and the approach companies should use.
- The fact that projects with positive NPVs theoretically increase the value of the company and the value of its stock could explain the use and popularity of the NPV method by companies.
- Real options allow companies to make future decisions contingent on future economic information or events that change the value of capital investment decisions the company has made today. These can be classified as (1) timing options; (2) sizing options, which can be abandonment options or growth (expansion) options; (3) flexibility options, which can be price-setting options or production-flexibility options; and (4) fundamental options.

PRACTICE PROBLEMS

1. With regard to capital allocation, an appropriate estimate of the incremental cash flows from an investment is *least likely* to include:
   A. externalities.

   B. interest costs.

   C. opportunity costs.

2. The NPV of an investment is equal to the sum of the expected cash flows discounted at the:

   A. internal rate of return.

   B. risk-free rate.

   C. opportunity COC.

3. A USD2.2 million investment will result in the following year-end cash flows:

Year	1	2	3	4
Cash flow (millions)	USD1.3	USD1.6	USD1.9	USD0.8

Using an 8% opportunity COC, the investment's NPV is *closest* to:

   A. USD2.47 million.

   B. USD3.40 million.

   C. USD4.67 million.

4. The IRR is *best* described as the:

   A. opportunity COC.

   B. time-weighted rate of return.

   C. discount rate that makes the NPV equal to zero.

5. A three-year investment requires an initial outlay of GBP1,000. It is expected to provide three year-end cash flows of GBP200 plus a net salvage value of GBP700 at the end of three years. Its IRR is *closest* to:

   A. 10%.

   B. 11%.

   C. 20%.

6. Given the following cash flows for a capital investment, calculate the NPV and IRR. The required rate of return is 8%.

Year	0	1	2	3	4	5
Cash flow	−50,000	15,000	15,000	20,000	10,000	5,000

	NPV	IRR
A	USD1,905	10.9%
B	USD1,905	26.0%
C	USD3,379	10.9%

7. An investment of USD100 generates after-tax cash flows of USD40 in Year 1, USD80 in Year 2, and USD120 in Year 3. The required rate of return is 20%. The NPV is *closest* to:

   A. USD42.22.

      B. USD58.33.
      C. USD68.52.

8. An investment of USD150,000 is expected to generate an after-tax cash flow of USD100,000 in one year and another USD120,000 in two years. The COC is 10%. What is the IRR?
    A. 28.39%
    B. 28.59%
    C. 28.79%

9. Kim Corporation is considering an investment of KRW750 million with expected after-tax cash inflows of KRW175 million per year for seven years. The required rate of return is 10%. What is the investment's:

	NPV?	IRR?
A.	KRW102 million	14.0%
B.	KRW157 million	23.3%
C.	KRW193 million	10.0%

10. Erin Chou is reviewing a profitable investment that has a conventional cash flow pattern. If the cash flows for the initial outlay and future after-tax cash flows all double, Chou would predict that the IRR would:
    A. increase and the NPV would increase.
    B. stay the same and the NPV would increase.
    C. stay the same and the NPV would stay the same.

11. Catherine Ndereba is an energy analyst tasked with evaluating a crude oil exploration and production company. The company previously announced that it plans to embark on a new project to drill for oil offshore. As a result of this announcement, the stock price increased by 10%. After conducting her analysis, Ms. Ndereba concludes that the project does indeed have a positive NPV. Which statement is true?
    A. The stock price should remain where it is because Ms. Ndereba's analysis confirms that the recent run-up was justified.
    B. The stock price should go even higher now that an independent source has confirmed that the NPV is positive.
    C. The stock price could remain steady, move higher, or move lower.

12. The Bearing Corp. invests only in positive-NPV projects. Which of the following statements is true?
    A. Bearing's ROIC is greater than its COC.
    B. Bearing's COC is greater than its ROIC.
    C. We cannot reach any conclusions about the relationship between the company's ROIC and COC.

13. Investments 1 and 2 have similar outlays, although the patterns of future cash flows are different. The cash flows, as well as the NPV and IRR, for the two investments are shown below. For both investments, the required rate of return is 10%.

	Cash Flows						
Year	0	1	2	3	4	NPV	IRR (%)
Investment 1	−50	20	20	20	20	13.40	21.86
Investment 2	−50	0	0	0	100	18.30	18.92

The two projects are mutually exclusive. What is the appropriate investment decision?
A. Invest in both investments.
B. Invest in Investment 1 because it has the higher IRR.
C. Invest in Investment 2 because it has the higher NPV.

14. Consider the two investments below. The cash flows, as well as the NPV and IRR, for the two investments are given. For both investments, the required rate of return is 10%.

	Cash Flows						
Year	0	1	2	3	4	NPV	IRR (%)
Investment 1	−100	36	36	36	36	14.12	16.37
Investment 2	−100	0	0	0	175	19.53	15.02

What discount rate would result in the same NPV for both investments?
A. A rate between 0.00% and 10.00%
B. A rate between 10.00% and 15.02%
C. A rate between 15.02% and 16.37%

15. Wilson Flannery is concerned that the following investment has multiple IRRs.

Year	0	1	2	3w
Cash flows	−50	100	0	−50

How many discount rates produce a zero NPV for this investment?
A. One, a discount rate of 0%
B. Two, discount rates of 0% and 32%
C. Two, discount rates of 0% and 62%

16. What type of project is *most likely* to yield new revenues for a company?
A. Regulatory/compliance
B. Going concern
C. Expansion

The following information relates to questions 17–19

Bouchard Industries is a Canadian company that manufactures gutters for residential houses. Its management believes it has developed a new process that produces a superior product. The company must make an initial investment of CAD190 million to begin production. If demand is high, cash flows are expected to be CAD40 million per year. If demand is low, cash flows will be only CAD20 million per year. Management believes there is an equal chance that demand will be high or low. The investment, which has an investment horizon of ten years, also gives the company a production-flexibility option allowing the company to add shifts at the end of the first year if demand turns out to be high. If the company exercises this option, net cash flows would increase by an additional CAD5 million in Years 2–10. Bouchard's opportunity cost of funds is 10%.

The internal auditor for Bouchard Industries has made two suggestions for improving capital allocation processes at the company. The internal auditor's suggestions are as follows:

Suggestion 1: "In order to treat all capital allocation proposals in a fair manner, the investments should all use the risk-free rate for the required rate of return."

Suggestion 2: "When rationing capital, it is better to choose the portfolio of investments that maximizes the company NPV than the portfolio that maximizes the company IRR."

17. What is the NPV (CAD millions) of the original project for Bouchard Industries without considering the production-flexibility option?
    A. –CAD6.11 million
    B. –CAD5.66 million
    C. CAD2.33 million

18. What is the NPV (CAD millions) of the optimal set of investment decisions for Bouchard Industries including the production-flexibility option?
    A. –CAD6.34 million
    B. CAD7.43 million
    C. CAD31.03 million

19. Should the capital allocation committee accept the internal auditor's suggestions?
    A. No for Suggestions 1 and 2
    B. No for Suggestion 1 and yes for Suggestion 2
    C. Yes for Suggestion 1 and no for Suggestion 2

CHAPTER 5

CAPITAL STRUCTURE

LEARNING OUTCOMES

The candidate should be able to:

- explain factors affecting capital structure
- describe how a company's capital structure may change over its life cycle
- explain the Modigliani–Miller propositions regarding capital structure
- describe the use of target capital structure in estimating WACC, and calculate and interpret target capital structure weights
- describe competing stakeholder interests in capital structure decisions

SUMMARY

- Financing decisions are typically tied to investment spending and are based on the company's ability to support debt given the nature of its business model, assets, and operating cash flows.
- A company's stage in the life cycle, its cash flow characteristics, and its ability to support debt largely dictate its capital structure, since capital not sourced through borrowing must come from equity (including retained earnings).
- Generally speaking, as companies mature and move from start-up through growth to maturity, their business risk declines as operating cash flows turn positive with increasing predictability, allowing for greater use of leverage on more attractive terms.
- Modigliani and Miller's work, with its simplifying assumptions, provides a starting point for thinking about the strategic use of debt and shows us that managers cannot change firm value simply by changing the firm's capital structure. Firm value is independent of capital structure decisions.
- Given the tax-deductibility of interest, adding leverage increases firm value up to a point but also increases the risk of default for capital providers who demand higher returns in compensation.
- To maximize firm value, management should target the optimal capital structure that minimizes the company's weighted average cost of capital.
- "Optimal capital structure" involves a trade-off between the benefits of higher leverage, which include the tax-deductibility of interest and the lower cost of debt relative to equity,

and the costs of higher leverage, which include higher risk for all capital providers and the potential costs of financial distress.

- Managers may provide investors with information ("signaling") through their choice of financing method. For example, commitments to fixed payments may signal management's confidence in the company's prospects.
- Managers' capital structure decisions impact various stakeholder groups differently. In seeking to maximize shareholder wealth or their own, managers may create conflicts of interest in which one or more groups are favored at the expense of others, such as a debt-equity conflict.

PRACTICE PROBLEMS

1. Which of the following is *least* likely to affect the capital structure of Longdrive Trucking Company? Longdrive has moderate leverage today.
   A. The acquisition of a major competitor for shares
   B. A substantial increase in share price
   C. The payment of a stock dividend

2. Which of these statements is *most* accurate with respect to the use of debt by a start-up fashion retailer with negative cash flow and uncertain revenue prospects?
   A. Debt financing will be unavailable or very costly.
   B. The company will prefer to use equity rather than debt given its uncertain cash flow outlook.
   C. Both A and B.

3. Which of the following is true of the growth stage in a company's development?
   A. Cash flow is negative, by definition, with investment outlays exceeding cash flow from operations.
   B. Cash flow may be negative or positive.
   C. Cash flow is positive and growing quickly.

4. Which of the following mature companies is *most* likely to use a high proportion of debt in its capital structure?
   A. A mining company with a large, fixed asset base
   B. A software company with very stable and predictable revenues and an asset-light business model
   C. An electric utility

5. Which of the following is *most* likely to occur as a company evolves from growth stage to maturity and seeks to optimize its capital structure?
   A. The company relies on equity to finance its growth.
   B. Leverage increases as the company needs more capital to support organic expansion.
   C. Leverage increases as the company is able to support more debt.

6. If investors have homogeneous expectations, the market is efficient, and there are no taxes, no transaction costs, and no bankruptcy costs, Modigliani and Miller's Proposition I states that:

    A. bankruptcy risk rises with more leverage.

    B. managers cannot change the value of the company by changing the amount of debt.

    C. managers cannot increase the value of the company by using tax-saving strategies.

7. According to Modigliani and Miller's Proposition II without taxes:

    A. the capital structure decision has no effect on the cost of equity.

    B. investment and capital structure decisions are interdependent.

    C. the cost of equity increases as the use of debt in the capital structure increases.

8. The weighted average cost of capital (WACC) for Van der Welde is 10%. The company announces a debt offering that raises the WACC to 13%. The *most* likely conclusion is that for Van der Welde:

    A. the company's prospects are improving.

    B. equity financing is cheaper than debt financing.

    C. the company's debt/equity has moved beyond the optimal range.

9. According to the static trade-off theory:

    A. debt should be used only as a last resort.

    B. companies have an optimal level of debt.

    C. the capital structure decision is irrelevant.

The following information relates to questions 10–12

Nailah Mablevi is an equity analyst who covers the entertainment industry for Kwame Capital Partners, a major global asset manager. Kwame owns a significant position, with a large unrealized capital gain, in Mosi Broadcast Group (MBG). On a recent conference call, MBG's management stated that they plan to increase the proportion of debt in the company's capital structure. Mablevi is concerned that any changes in MBG's capital structure will negatively affect the value of Kwame's investment.

    To evaluate the potential impact of such a capital structure change on Kwame's investment, she gathers the information about MBG given in Exhibit 1.

EXHIBIT 1: Current Selected Financial Information on MBG

Yield to maturity on debt	8.00%
Market value of debt	USD100 million
Number of shares of common stock	10 million
Market price per share of common stock	USD30
Cost of capital if all equity-financed	10.3%
Marginal tax rate	35%

10. MBG is *best* described as currently:

    A. 25% debt-financed and 75% equity-financed.

    B. 33% debt-financed and 66% equity-financed.

    C. 75% debt-financed and 25% equity-financed.

11. Holding operating earnings constant, an increase in the marginal tax rate to 40% would:
    A. result in a lower cost of debt capital.
    B. result in a higher cost of debt capital.
    C. not affect the company's cost of capital.

12. Which of the following is *least* likely to be true with respect to optimal capital structure?
    A. The optimal capital structure minimizes WACC.
    B. The optimal capital structure is generally close to the target capital structure.
    C. Debt can be a significant portion of the optimal capital structure because of the tax-deductibility of interest.

13. Other factors being equal, in which of the following situations are debt-equity conflicts likely to arise?
    A. Financial leverage is low.
    B. The company's debt is secured.
    C. The company's debt is long-term.

14. Which of the following is an example of agency costs? In each case, management is advocating a substantial acquisition and management compensation is heavily composed of stock options.
    A. Management believes the acquisition will be positive for shareholder value but negative for the value and interests of the company's debtholders.
    B. Management's stock options are worthless at the current share price. The acquisition has a high (50%) risk of failure (with zero value) but substantial (30%) upside if it works out.
    C. The acquisition is positive for equityholders and does not significantly impair the position of debtholders. However, the acquisition puts the company into a new business where labor practices are harsh and the production process is environmentally damaging.

15. Which of the following is *least* accurate with respect to debt-equity conflicts?
    A. Equityholders focus on potential upside and downside outcomes, while debtholders focus primarily on downside risk.
    B. Management attempts to balance the interests of equityholders and debtholders.
    C. Debt covenants can mitigate the conflict between debtholders and equityholders.

16. Which of the following is *least* likely to be true with respect to agency costs and senior management compensation?
    A. Equity-based incentive compensation is the primary method to address the problem of agency costs.
    B. A well-designed compensation scheme should eliminate agency costs.
    C. High cash compensation for senior management, without significant equity-based performance incentives, can lead to excessive caution and complacency.

17. Integrated Systems Solutions Inc. (ISS) is a technology company that sells software to companies in the building construction industry. The company's assets consist mostly of intangible assets. Although the company is profitable, revenue growth and earnings growth have been slowing in recent years. The company's business model is a pay-per-use model, and given the cyclical nature of the construction industry, the company's revenues and earnings vary considerably over the business cycle.

Describe two factors that would point to ISS having a relatively high cost of borrowing and low proportion of debt in its capital structure.

18. Tillett Technologies is a manufacturer of high-end audio and video (AV) equipment. The company, with no debt in its capital structure, has experienced rapid growth in revenues and improved profitability in recent years. About half of the company's revenues come from subscription-based service agreements. The company's assets consist mostly of inventory and property, plant, and equipment, representing its production facilities. Now, the company seeks to raise new capital to finance additional growth.

    Describe two factors that would support Tillett being able to access debt capital at a reasonable cost to finance the additional growth. Justify your response.

19. Discuss two financial metrics that can be used to assess a company's ability to service additional debt in its capital structure.

20. Identify two market conditions that can be characterized as favorable for companies wishing to add debt to their capital structures.

21. Which of the following is *least* accurate with respect to the market value and book value of a company's equity?
    A. Market value is more relevant than book value when measuring a company's cost of capital.
    B. Book value is often used by lenders and in financial ratio calculations.
    C. Both market value and book value fluctuate with changes in the company's share price.

22. Fran McClure of Alba Advisers is estimating the cost of capital of Frontier Corporation as part of her valuation analysis of Frontier. McClure will be using this estimate, along with projected cash flows from Frontier's new projects, to estimate the effect of these new projects on the value of Frontier. McClure has gathered the following information on Frontier Corporation:

	Current Year (USD)	Forecasted for Next Year (USD)
Book value of debt	50	50
Market value of debt	62	63
Book value of shareholders' equity	55	58
Market value of shareholders' equity	210	220

The weights that McClure should apply in estimating Frontier's cost of capital for debt and equity are, respectively:
A. $w_d = 0.200$; $w_e = 0.800$.
B. $w_d = 0.185$; $w_e = 0.815$.
C. $w_d = 0.223$; $w_e = 0.777$.

23. Which of the following is *not* a reason why target capital structure and actual capital structure tend to differ?
    A. Financing is often tied to a specific investment.
    B. Companies raise capital when the terms are attractive.
    C. Target capital structure is set for a particular project, while actual capital structure is measured at the consolidated company level.

24. According to the pecking order theory:
    A. new debt is preferable to new equity.
    B. new debt is preferable to internally generated funds.
    C. new equity is always preferable to other sources of capital.

25. Vega Company has announced that it intends to raise capital next year, but it is unsure as to the appropriate method of raising capital. White, the CFO, has concluded that Vega should apply the pecking order theory to determine the appropriate method of raising capital. Based on White's conclusion, Vega should raise capital in the following order:
    A. debt, internal financing, equity.
    B. equity, debt, internal financing.
    C. internal financing, debt, equity.

CHAPTER 6

MEASURES OF LEVERAGE

LEARNING OUTCOMES

The candidate should be able to:

- define and explain leverage, business risk, sales risk, operating risk, and financial risk and classify a risk
- calculate and interpret the degree of operating leverage, the degree of financial leverage, and the degree of total leverage
- analyze the effect of financial leverage on a company's net income and return on equity
- calculate the breakeven quantity of sales and determine the company's net income at various sales levels
- calculate and interpret the operating breakeven quantity of sales

SUMMARY

In this chapter, we have reviewed the fundamentals of business risk, financial risk, and measures of leverage.

- Leverage is the use of fixed costs in a company's cost structure. Business risk is the risk associated with operating earnings and reflects both sales risk (uncertainty with respect to the price and quantity of sales) and operating risk (the risk related to the use of fixed costs in operations). Financial risk is the risk associated with how a company finances its operations (i.e., the split between equity and debt financing of the business).
- The degree of operating leverage (DOL) is the ratio of the percentage change in operating income to the percentage change in units sold. We can use the following formula to measure the degree of operating leverage:

$$DOL = \frac{Q(P - V)}{Q(P - V) - F}$$

- The degree of financial leverage (DFL) is the percentage change in net income for a one percent change in operating income. We can use the following formula to measure the degree of financial leverage:

$$\text{DFL} = \frac{[Q(P-V)-F](1-t)}{[Q(P-V)-F-C](1-t)} = \frac{[Q(P-V)-F]}{[Q(P-V)-F-C]}$$

- The degree of total leverage (DTL) is a measure of the sensitivity of net income to changes in unit sales, which is equivalent to DTL = DOL × DFL.
- The breakeven point, Q_{BE}, is the number of units produced and sold at which the company's net income is zero, which we calculate as

$$Q_{BE} = \frac{F+C}{P-V}$$

- The operating breakeven point, Q_{OBE}, is the number of units produced and sold at which the company's operating income is zero, which we calculate as

$$Q_{OBE} = \frac{F}{P-V}$$

PRACTICE PROBLEMS

The following information relates to questions 1–9

Mary Benn, CFA, is a financial analyst for Twin Fields Investments, located in Storrs, Connecticut, USA. She has been asked by her supervisor, Bill Cho, to examine two small Japanese cell phone component manufacturers: 4G, Inc. and Qphone Corp. Cho indicates that his clients are most interested in the use of leverage by 4G and Qphone. Benn states, "I will have to specifically analyze each company's respective business risk, sales risk, operating risk, and financial risk." "Fine, I'll check back with you shortly," Cho, answers.

Benn begins her analysis by examining the sales prospects of the two firms. The results of her sales analysis appear in Exhibit 1. She also expects very little price variability for these cell phones. She next gathers more data on these two companies to assist her analysis of their operating and financial risk.

When Cho inquires as to her progress Benn responds, "I have calculated Qphone's degree of operating leverage (DOL) and degree of financial leverage (DFL) at Qphone's 2009 level of unit sales. I have also calculated Qphone's breakeven level for unit sales. I will have 4G's leverage results shortly."

Cho responds, "Good, I will call a meeting of some potential investors for tomorrow. Please help me explain these concepts to them, and the differences in use of leverage by these two companies. In preparation for the meeting, I have a number of questions":

- "You mentioned business risk; what is included in that?"
- "How would you classify the risk due to the varying mix of variable and fixed costs?"
- "Could you conduct an analysis and tell me how the two companies will fare relative to each other in terms of net income if their unit sales increased by 10 percent above their 2009 unit sales levels?"

- "Finally, what would be an accurate verbal description of the degree of total leverage?"

The relevant data for analysis of 4G is contained in Exhibit 2, and Benn's analysis of the Qphone data appears in Exhibit 3:

EXHIBIT 1: Benn's Unit Sales Estimates for 4G, Inc. and Qphone Corp.

Company	2009 Unit Sales	Standard Deviation of Unit Sales	2010 Expected Unit Sales Growth Rate (%)
4G, Inc.	1,000,000	25,000	15
Qphone Corp.	1,500,000	10,000	15

EXHIBIT 2: Sales, Cost, and Expense Data for 4G, Inc. (At Unit Sales of 1,000,000)

Number of units produced and sold	1,000,000
Sales price per unit	¥108
Variable cost per unit	¥72
Fixed operating cost	¥22,500,000
Fixed financing expense	¥9,000,000

EXHIBIT 3: Benn's Analysis of Qphone (At Unit Sales of 1,500,000)

Degree of operating leverage	1.40
Degree of financial leverage	1.15
Breakeven quantity (units)	571,429

1. Based on Benn's analysis, 4G's sales risk relative to Qphone's is *most likely* to be:
   A. lower.
   B. equal.
   C. higher.

2. What is the *most appropriate* response to Cho's question regarding the components of business risk?
   A. Sales risk and financial risk.
   B. Operating risk and sales risk.
   C. Financial risk and operating risk.

3. The *most appropriate* response to Cho's question regarding the classification of risk arising from the mixture of variable and fixed costs is:
   A. sales risk.
   B. financial risk.
   C. operating risk.

4. Based on the information in Exhibit 2, the degree of operating leverage (DOL) of 4G, Inc., at unit sales of 1,000,000, is *closest* to:
   A. 1.60.
   B. 2.67.
   C. 3.20.

5. Based on the information in Exhibit 2, 4G, Inc.'s degree of financial leverage (DFL), at unit sales of 1,000,000, is *closest* to:
   A. 1.33.
   B. 2.67.
   C. 3.00.

6. Based on the information in Exhibit 1 and Exhibit 3, Qphone's expected percentage change in operating income for 2010 is *closest* to:
   A. 17.25%.
   B. 21.00%.
   C. 24.30%.

7. 4G's breakeven quantity of unit sales is *closest* to:
   A. 437,500 units.
   B. 625,000 units.
   C. 875,000 units.

8. In response to Cho's question regarding an increase in unit sales above 2009 unit sales levels, it is *most likely* that 4G's net income will increase at:
   A. a slower rate than Qphone's.
   B. the same rate as Qphone's.
   C. a faster rate than Qphone's.

9. The *most appropriate* response to Cho's question regarding a description of the degree of total leverage is that degree of total leverage is:
   A. the percentage change in net income divided by the percentage change in units sold.
   B. the percentage change in operating income divided by the percentage change in units sold.
   C. the percentage change in net income divided by the percentage change in operating income.

10. If two companies have identical unit sales volume and operating risk, they are *most likely* to also have identical:
    A. sales risk.
    B. business risk.
    C. sensitivity of operating earnings to changes in the number of units produced and sold.

11. Degree of operating leverage is *best* described as a measure of the sensitivity of:
    A. net earnings to changes in sales.
    B. fixed operating costs to changes in variable costs.
    C. operating earnings to changes in the number of units produced and sold.

12. The Fulcrum Company produces decorative swivel platforms for home televisions. If Fulcrum produces 40 million units, it estimates that it can sell them for $100 each.

Variable production costs are $65 per unit and fixed production costs are $1.05 billion. Which of the following statements is *most accurate*? Holding all else constant, the Fulcrum Company would:

A. generate positive operating income if unit sales were 25 million.
B. have less operating leverage if fixed production costs were 10 percent greater than $1.05 billion.
C. generate 20 percent more operating income if unit sales were 5 percent greater than 40 million.

13. The business risk of a particular company is *most accurately* measured by the company's:
    A. debt-to-equity ratio.
    B. efficiency in using assets to generate sales.
    C. operating leverage and level of uncertainty about demand, output prices, and competition.

14. Consider two companies that operate in the same line of business and have the same degree of operating leverage: the Basic Company and the Grundlegend Company. The Basic Company and the Grundlegend Company have, respectively, no debt and 50 percent debt in their capital structure. Which of the following statements is *most accurate*? Compared to the Basic Company, the Grundlegend Company has:
    A. a lower sensitivity of net income to changes in unit sales.
    B. the same sensitivity of operating income to changes in unit sales.
    C. the same sensitivity of net income to changes in operating income.

15. Myundia Motors now sells 1 million units at ¥3,529 per unit. Fixed operating costs are ¥1,290 million and variable operating costs are ¥1,500 per unit. If the company pays ¥410 million in interest, the levels of sales at the operating breakeven and breakeven points are, respectively:
    A. ¥1,500,000,000 and ¥2,257,612,900.
    B. ¥2,243,671,760 and ¥2,956,776,737.
    C. ¥2,975,148,800 and ¥3,529,000,000.

16. Juan Alavanca is evaluating the risk of two companies in the machinery industry: The Gearing Company and Hebelkraft, Inc. Alavanca used the latest fiscal year's financial statements and interviews with managers of the respective companies to gather the following information:

	The Gearing Company	Hebelkraft, Inc.
Number of units produced and sold	1 million	1.5 million
Sales price per unit	$200	$200
Variable cost per unit	$120	$100
Fixed operating cost	$40 million	$90 million
Fixed financing expense	$20 million	$20 million

Based on this information, the breakeven points for The Gearing Company and Hebelkraft, Inc. are:

A. 0.75 million and 1.1 million units, respectively.
B. 1 million and 1.5 million units, respectively.
C. 1.5 million and 0.75 million units, respectively.

CHAPTER 7

COST OF CAPITAL: FOUNDATIONAL TOPICS

LEARNING OUTCOMES

The candidate should be able to:

- calculate and interpret the weighted average cost of capital (WACC) of a company
- describe how taxes affect the cost of capital from different capital sources
- calculate and interpret the cost of debt capital using the yield-to-maturity approach and the debt-rating approach
- calculate and interpret the cost of noncallable, nonconvertible preferred stock
- calculate and interpret the cost of equity capital using the capital asset pricing model approach and the bond yield plus risk premium approach
- explain and demonstrate beta estimation for public companies, thinly traded public companies, and nonpublic companies
- explain and demonstrate the correct treatment of flotation costs

SUMMARY

In this chapter, we provided an overview of the techniques used to calculate the cost of capital for companies and projects. We examined the weighted average cost of capital, discussing the methods commonly used to estimate the component costs of capital and the weights applied to these components.

- The weighted average cost of capital is a weighted average of the after-tax marginal costs of each source of capital: $\text{WACC} = w_d r_d (1 - t) + w_p r_p + w_e r_e$.
- The before-tax cost of debt is generally estimated by either the yield-to-maturity method or the bond rating method.
- The yield-to-maturity method of estimating the before-tax cost of debt uses the familiar bond valuation equation. Assuming semi-annual coupon payments, the equation is

$$P_0 = \frac{PMT_1}{\left(1 + \frac{r_d}{2}\right)} + \ldots + \frac{PMT_n}{\left(1 + \frac{r_d}{2}\right)^n} + \frac{FV}{\left(1 + \frac{r_d}{2}\right)^n} = \left[\sum_{t=1}^{n} \frac{PMT_t}{\left(1 + \frac{r_d}{2}\right)^t}\right] + \frac{FV}{\left(1 + \frac{r_d}{2}\right)^n}.$$

We solve for the six-month yield $(r_d/2)$ and then annualize it to arrive at the before-tax cost of debt, r_d.

- Because interest payments are generally tax deductible, the after-tax cost is the true, effective cost of debt to the company. If a yield to maturity or bond rating is not available, such as in the case of a private company without rated debt or a project, the estimate of the cost of debt becomes more challenging.
- The cost of preferred stock is the preferred stock dividend divided by the current preferred stock price:

$$r_p = \frac{D_p}{P_p}.$$

- The cost of equity is the rate of return required by a company's common stockholders. We estimate this cost using the CAPM (or its variants).
- The CAPM is the approach most commonly used to calculate the cost of equity. The three components needed to calculate the cost of equity are the risk-free rate, the equity risk premium, and beta:

$$E(R_i) = R_F + \beta_i[E(R_M) - R_F].$$

- In estimating the cost of equity, an alternative to the CAPM is the bond yield plus risk premium approach. In this approach, we estimate the before-tax cost of debt and add a risk premium that reflects the additional risk associated with the company's equity.
- When estimating the cost of equity capital using the CAPM, if we do not have publicly traded equity, we may be able to use a comparable company operating in the same business line to estimate the unlevered beta for a company with similar business risk, β_U:

$$\beta_U = \beta_E\left[\frac{1}{1 + (1 - t)\frac{D}{E}}\right].$$

Then, we lever this beta to reflect the financial risk of the project or company:

$$\beta_E = \beta_U\left[1 + (1 - t)\frac{D}{E}\right].$$

- Flotation costs are costs incurred in the process of raising additional capital. The preferred method of including these costs in the analysis is as an initial cash flow in the valuation analysis.
- Survey evidence tells us that the CAPM method is the most popular method used by companies in estimating the cost of equity. The CAPM method is more popular with larger, publicly traded companies, which is understandable considering the additional analyses and assumptions required in estimating systematic risk for a private company or project.

PRACTICE PROBLEMS

The following information relates to questions 1–5

Jurgen Knudsen has been hired to provide industry expertise to Henrik Sandell, CFA, an analyst for a pension plan managing a global large-cap fund internally. Sandell is concerned about one of the fund's larger holdings, auto parts manufacturer Kruspa AB. Kruspa currently operates in 80 countries, with the previous year's global revenues at €5.6 billion. Recently, Kruspa's CFO announced plans for expansion into Trutan, a country with a developing economy. Sandell worries that this expansion will change the company's risk profile and wonders if he should recommend a sale of the position.

Sandell provides Knudsen with the basic information. Kruspa's global annual free cash flow to the firm is €500 million, and earnings are €400 million. Sandell estimates that cash flow will level off at a 2% rate of growth. Sandell also estimates that Kruspa's after-tax free cash flow to the firm on the Trutan project for the next three years is, respectively, €48 million, €52 million, and €54.4 million. Kruspa recently announced a dividend of €4.00 per share of stock. For the initial analysis, Sandell requests that Knudsen ignore possible currency fluctuations. He expects the Trutanese plant to sell only to customers within Trutan for the first three years. Knudsen is asked to evaluate Kruspa's planned financing of the required €100 million in Sweden with an €80 million public offering of 10-year debt and the remainder with an equity offering.

Additional Information	
Equity risk premium, Sweden	4.82%
Risk-free rate of interest, Sweden	4.25%
Industry debt-to-equity ratio	0.3
Market value of Kruspa's debt	€900 million
Market value of Kruspa's equity	€2.4 billion
Kruspa's equity beta	1.3
Kruspa's before-tax cost of debt	9.25%
Trutan credit A2 country risk premium	1.88%
Corporate tax rate	37.5%
Interest payments each year	Level

1. Using the capital asset pricing model, Kruspa's cost of equity capital for its typical project is *closest* to:
   A. 7.62%.
   B. 10.52%.
   C. 12.40%.

2. Sandell is interested in the weighted average cost of capital of Kruspa AB prior to its investing in the Trutan project. This weighted average cost of capital is *closest* to:
   A. 7.65%.
   B. 9.23%.
   C. 10.17%.

3. In his estimation of the project's cost of capital, Sandell would like to use the asset beta of Kruspa as a base in his calculations. The estimated asset beta of Kruspa prior to the Trutan project is *closest* to:
   A. 1.053.
   B. 1.110.
   C. 1.327.

4. Sandell is performing a sensitivity analysis of the effect of the new project on the company's cost of capital. If the Trutan project has the same asset risk as Kruspa, the estimated project beta for the Trutan project, if it is financed 80% with debt, is *closest* to:
   A. 1.300.
   B. 2.635.
   C. 3.686.

5. As part of the sensitivity analysis of the effect of the new project on the company's cost of capital, Sandell is estimating the cost of equity of the Trutan project considering that the Trutan project requires a country equity premium to capture the risk of the project. The cost of equity for the project in this case is *closest* to:
   A. 10.52%.
   B. 19.91%.
   C. 28.95%.

6. Which of the following statements is correct?
   A. The appropriate tax rate to use in the adjustment of the before-tax cost of debt to determine the after-tax cost of debt is the average tax rate because interest is deductible against the company's entire taxable income.
   B. For a given company, the after-tax cost of debt is generally less than both the cost of preferred equity and the cost of common equity.
   C. For a given company, the after-tax cost of debt is generally higher than both the cost of preferred equity and the cost of common equity.

7. The Gearing Company has an after-tax cost of debt capital of 4%, a cost of preferred stock of 8%, a cost of equity capital of 10%, and a weighted average cost of capital of 7%. Gearing intends to maintain its current capital structure as it raises additional capital. In making its capital-budgeting decisions for the average-risk project, the relevant cost of capital is:
   A. 4%.
   B. 7%.
   C. 8%.

8. Fran McClure, of Alba Advisers, is estimating the cost of capital of Frontier Corporation as part of her valuation analysis of Frontier. McClure will be using this estimate, along with projected cash flows from Frontier's new projects, to estimate the effect of these new projects on the value of Frontier. McClure has gathered the following information on Frontier Corporation:

	Current Year ($)	Forecasted for Next Year ($)
Book value of debt	50	50
Market value of debt	62	63
Book value of equity	55	58
Market value equity	210	220

The weights that McClure should apply in estimating Frontier's cost of capital for debt and equity are, respectively:
A. $w_d = 0.200$ and $w_e = 0.800$.
B. $w_d = 0.185$ and $w_e = 0.815$.
C. $w_d = 0.223$ and $w_e = 0.777$.

9. An analyst assembles the following facts concerning a company's component costs of capital and capital structure. Based on the information given, calculate the company's WACC.

Facts	(%)
Cost of equity based on the CAPM	15.60
Pretax cost of debt	8.28
Corporate tax rate	30.00
Capital structure weight	Equity 80, Debt 20

10. The cost of equity is equal to the:
    A. expected market return.
    B. rate of return required by stockholders.
    C. cost of retained earnings plus dividends.

11. Dot.Com has determined that it could issue $1,000 face value bonds with an 8% coupon paid semi-annually and a five-year maturity at $900 per bond. If Dot.Com's marginal tax rate is 38%, its after-tax cost of debt is *closest* to:
    A. 6.2%.
    B. 6.4%.
    C. 6.6%.

12. The cost of debt can be determined using the yield-to-maturity and bond rating approaches. If the bond rating approach is used, the:
    A. coupon is the yield.
    B. yield is based on the interest coverage ratio.
    C. company is rated and the rating can be used to assess the credit default spread of the company's debt.

13. Morgan Insurance Ltd. issued a fixed-rate perpetual preferred stock three years ago and placed it privately with institutional investors. The stock was issued at $25 per share with

a $1.75 dividend. If the company were to issue preferred stock today, the yield would be 6.5%. The stock's current value is:

A. $25.00.

B. $26.92.

C. $37.31.

14. Two years ago, a company issued $20 million in long-term bonds at par value with a coupon rate of 9%. The company has decided to issue an additional $20 million in bonds and expects the new issue to be priced at par value with a coupon rate of 7%. The company has no other debt outstanding and has a tax rate of 40%. To compute the company's weighted average cost of capital, the appropriate after-tax cost of debt is *closest* to:

A. 4.2%.

B. 4.8%.

C. 5.4%.

15. At the time of valuation, the estimated betas for JPMorgan Chase & Co. and the Boeing Company were 1.50 and 0.80, respectively. The risk-free rate of return was 4.35%, and the equity risk premium was 8.04%. Based on these data, calculate the required rates of return for these two stocks using the CAPM.

16. An analyst's data source shows that Newmont Mining (NEM) has an estimated beta of −0.2. The risk-free rate of return is 2.5%, and the equity risk premium is estimated to be 4.5%.

A. Using the CAPM, calculate the required rate of return for investors in NEM.

B. The analyst notes that the current yield to maturity on corporate bonds with a credit rating similar to NEM is approximately 3.9%. How should this information affect the analyst's estimate?

17. Wang Securities had a long-term stable debt-to-equity ratio of 0.65. Recent bank borrowing for expansion into South America raised the ratio to 0.75. The increased leverage has what effect on the asset beta and equity beta of the company?

A. The asset beta and the equity beta will both rise.

B. The asset beta will remain the same, and the equity beta will rise.

C. The asset beta will remain the same, and the equity beta will decline.

18. Brandon Wiene is a financial analyst covering the beverage industry. He is evaluating the impact of DEF Beverage's new product line of flavored waters. DEF currently has a debt-to-equity ratio of 0.6. The new product line would be financed with $50 million of debt and $100 million of equity. In estimating the valuation impact of this new product line on DEF's value, Wiene has estimated the equity beta and asset beta of comparable companies. In calculating the equity beta for the product line, Wiene is intending to use DEF's existing capital structure when converting the asset beta into a project beta. Which of the following statements is correct?

A. Using DEF's debt-to-equity ratio of 0.6 is appropriate in calculating the new product line's equity beta.

B. Using DEF's debt-to-equity ratio of 0.6 is not appropriate; rather, the debt-to-equity ratio of the new product, 0.5, is appropriate to use in calculating the new product line's equity beta.

C. Wiene should use the new debt-to-equity ratio of DEF that would result from the additional $50 million debt and $100 million equity in calculating the new product line's equity beta.

19. Happy Resorts Company currently has 1.2 million common shares of stock outstanding, and the stock has a beta of 2.2. It also has $10 million face value of bonds that have five years remaining to maturity and an 8% coupon with semi-annual payments and are priced to yield 13.65%. If Happy issues up to $2.5 million of new bonds, the bonds will be priced at par and will have a yield of 13.65%; if it issues bonds beyond $2.5 million, the expected yield on the entire issuance will be 16%. Happy has learned that it can issue new common stock at $10 a share. The current risk-free rate of interest is 3%, and the expected market return is 10%. Happy's marginal tax rate is 30%. If Happy raises $7.5 million of new capital while maintaining the same debt-to-equity ratio, its weighted average cost of capital will be *closest* to:
   A. 14.5%.
   B. 15.5%.
   C. 16.5%.

The following information relates to questions 20–23
Boris Duarte, CFA, covers initial public offerings for Zellweger Analytics, an independent research firm specializing in global small-cap equities. He has been asked to evaluate the upcoming new issue of TagOn, a US-based business intelligence software company. The industry has grown at 26% per year for the previous three years. Large companies dominate the market, but sizable comparable companies, such as Relevant Ltd., ABJ Inc., and Opus Software Pvt. Ltd., also compete. Each of these competitors is domiciled in a different country, but they all have shares of stock that trade on the US NASDAQ. The debt ratio of the industry has risen slightly in recent years.

Company	Sales in Millions ($)	Market Value Equity in Millions ($)	Market Value Debt in Millions ($)	Equity Beta	Tax Rate (%)	Share Price ($)
Relevant Ltd.	752	3,800	0.0	1.702	23	42
ABJ Inc.	843	2,150	6.5	2.800	23	24
Opus Software Pvt. Ltd.	211	972	13.0	3.400	23	13

Duarte uses the information from the preliminary prospectus for TagOn's initial offering. The company intends to issue 1 million new shares. In his conversation with the investment bankers for the deal, he concludes the offering price will be between $7 and $12. The current capital structure of TagOn consists of a $2.4 million five-year noncallable bond issue and 1 million common shares. The following table includes other information that Duarte has gathered:

Currently outstanding bonds	$2.4 million five-year bonds, coupon of 12.5% paying semi-annually with a market value of $2.156 million
Risk-free rate of interest	5.25%
Estimated equity risk premium	7%
Tax rate	23%

20. The asset betas for Relevant, ABJ, and Opus, respectively, are:
   A. 1.70, 2.52, and 2.73.
   B. 1.70, 2.79, and 3.37.
   C. 1.70, 2.81, and 3.44.

21. The average asset beta for comparable players in this industry, Relevant, ABJ, and Opus, weighted by market value of equity is *closest* to:
   A. 1.67.
   B. 1.97.
   C. 2.27.

22. Using the capital asset pricing model, the cost of equity capital for a company in this industry with a debt-to-equity ratio of 0.01, an asset beta of 2.27, and a marginal tax rate of 23% is *closest* to:
   A. 17%.
   B. 21%.
   C. 24%.

23. The marginal cost of capital for TagOn, based on an average asset beta of 2.27 for the industry and assuming that new stock can be issued at $8 per share, is *closest* to:
   A. 20.5%.
   B. 21.0%.
   C. 21.5%.

24. An analyst gathered the following information about a private company and its publicly traded competitor:

Comparable Companies	Tax Rate (%)	Debt/Equity	Equity Beta
Private company	30.0	1.00	na
Public company	35.0	0.90	1.75

The estimated equity beta for the private company is *closest* to:
   A. 1.029.
   B. 1.104.
   C. 1.877.

25. Which of the following statements is *most accurate*? If two equity issues have the same market risk but the first issue has higher leverage, greater liquidity, and a higher required return, the higher required return *is most likely* the result of the first issue's:
   A. greater liquidity.
   B. higher leverage.
   C. higher leverage and greater liquidity.

26. SebCoe plc, a British firm, is evaluating an investment in a £50 million project that will be financed with 50% debt and 50% equity. Management has already determined that the NPV of this project is £5 million if it uses internally generated equity. However, if

the company uses external equity, it will incur flotation costs of 5.8%. Assuming flotation costs are not tax deductible, the NPV using external equity would be:

A. less than £5 million because we would discount the cash flows using a higher weighted average cost of capital that reflects the flotation costs.

B. £3.55 million because flotation costs reduce NPV by $1.45 million.

C. £5 million because flotation costs have no impact on NPV.

CHAPTER 8

COST OF CAPITAL: ADVANCED TOPICS

LEARNING OUTCOMES

The candidate should be able to:

- explain top-down and bottom-up factors that impact the cost of capital
- compare methods used to estimate the cost of debt.
- explain historical and forward-looking approaches to estimating an equity risk premium
- compare methods used to estimate the required return on equity
- estimate the cost of debt or required return on equity for a public company and a private company
- evaluate a company's capital structure and cost of capital relative to peers

PRACTICE PROBLEMS

1. Calculate an estimate of Precision's after-tax cost of debt.

2. Explain why the SP LM chose for estimating Precision's cost of equity is likely justified in being near the high end of the range.

3. Discuss company characteristics of Precision that would justify a higher or lower SCRP.

4. Calculate estimates of Precision's cost of equity using the (1) extended CAPM and the (2) build-up approach.

5. Calculate an estimate of Precision's WACC using the build-up approach estimate of the cost of equity.

The following information relates to questions 6–10

An equity index is established in Year 1 for a country that has recently moved to a market economy. The index vendor constructed returns for the four years prior to Year 1 based on the initial group of companies constituting the index in Year 1. From Year 12 to Year 16, a series of military confrontations concerning a disputed border disrupted the economy and financial markets. The dispute is conclusively arbitrated at the end of Year 16. In total,

20 years of equity market return history is available. Other selected data are in the following tables.

Selected Data

Geometric mean return relative to 10-year government bond returns (over a 20-year period)	2% per year
Arithmetic mean return relative to 10-year government bond returns (over a 20-year period)	2.3% per year
Index forward dividend yield	1%
Forecasted public company earnings growth	5% per year
Forecasted market P/E growth	1% per year
Forecasted real GDP growth rate (by Year 19)	4%
Current vs. long-term inflation forecast	6% vs. 4% per year
Current yield curve (inversion)	Short maturities: 9% 10-year maturities: 7%

6. The inclusion of index returns prior to Year 1 would be expected to:
   A. bias the historical ERP estimate upward.
   B. bias the historical ERP estimate downward.
   C. have no effect on the historical ERP estimate.

7. The events of 2012 to 2016 would be expected to:
   A. bias the historical ERP estimate upward.
   B. bias the historical ERP estimate downward.
   C. have no effect on the historical ERP estimate.

8. In the current interest rate environment, using a required return on equity estimate based on the short-term government bond rate and a historical ERP defined in terms of a short-term government bond rate would be expected to:
   A. bias long-term required return on equity estimates upward.
   B. bias long-term required return on equity estimates downward.
   C. have no effect on long-term required return on equity estimates.

9. An estimate of the ERP consistent with the Grinold-Kroner model is *closest* to:
   A. 2.7%.
   B. 3.0%.
   C. 4.3%.

10. Common stock issues in the aforementioned market with average systematic risk are *most likely* to have required rates of return of:
    A. between 2% and 7%.
    B. between 7% and 9%.
    C. 9% or greater.

CHAPTER 9

ANALYSIS OF DIVIDENDS AND SHARE REPURCHASES

LEARNING OUTCOMES

The candidate should be able to:

- describe the expected effect of regular cash dividends, extra dividends, liquidating dividends, stock dividends, stock splits, and reverse stock splits on shareholders' wealth and a company's financial ratios
- compare theories of dividend policy and explain implications of each for share value given a description of a corporate dividend action
- describe types of information (signals) that dividend initiations, increases, decreases, and omissions may convey
- explain how agency costs may affect a company's payout policy
- explain factors that affect dividend policy in practice
- calculate and interpret the effective tax rate on a given currency unit of corporate earnings under double taxation, dividend imputation, and split-rate tax systems
- compare stable dividend with constant dividend payout ratio, and calculate the dividend under each policy
- describe broad trends in corporate payout policies
- compare share repurchase methods
- calculate and compare the effect of a share repurchase on earnings per share when 1) the repurchase is financed with the company's surplus cash and 2) the company uses debt to finance the repurchase
- calculate the effect of a share repurchase on book value per share
- explain the choice between paying cash dividends and repurchasing shares
- calculate and interpret dividend coverage ratios based on 1) net income and 2) free cash flow
- identify characteristics of companies that may not be able to sustain their cash dividend

SUMMARY

A company's cash dividend payment and share repurchase policies constitute its payout policy. Both entail the distribution of the company's cash to its shareholders affect the form in which shareholders receive the return on their investment. Among the points this chapter has made are the following:

- Dividends can take the form of regular or irregular cash payments, stock dividends, or stock splits. Only cash dividends are payments to shareholders. Stock dividends and splits merely carve equity into smaller pieces and do not create wealth for shareholders. Reverse stock splits usually occur after a stock has dropped to a very low price and do not affect shareholder wealth.
- Regular cash dividends—unlike irregular cash dividends, stock splits, and stock dividends—represent a commitment to pay cash to stockholders on a quarterly, semiannual, or annual basis.
- There are three general theories on investor preference for dividends. The first, MM, argues that given perfect markets dividend policy is irrelevant. The second, "bird in hand" theory, contends that investors value a dollar of dividends today more than uncertain capital gains in the future. The third theory argues that in countries in which dividends are taxed at higher rates than capital gains, taxable investors prefer that companies reinvest earnings in profitable growth opportunities or repurchase shares so they receive more of the return in the form of capital gains.
- An argument for dividend irrelevance given perfect markets is that corporate dividend policy is irrelevant because shareholders can create their preferred cash flow stream by selling the company's shares ("homemade dividends").
- Dividend declarations may provide information to current and prospective shareholders regarding management's confidence in the prospects of the company. Initiating a dividend or increasing a dividend sends a positive signal, whereas cutting a dividend or omitting a dividend typically sends a negative signal. In addition, some institutional and individual shareholders see regular cash dividend payments as a measure of investment quality.
- Payment of dividends can help reduce the agency conflicts between managers and shareholders, but it also can worsen conflicts of interest between shareholders and debtholders.
- Empirically, several factors appear to influence dividend policy, including investment opportunities for the company, the volatility expected in its future earnings, financial flexibility, tax considerations, flotation costs, and contractual and legal restrictions.
- Under double taxation systems, dividends are taxed at both the corporate and shareholder level. Under tax imputation systems, a shareholder receives a tax credit on dividends for the tax paid on corporate profits. Under split-rate taxation systems, corporate profits are taxed at different rates depending on whether the profits are retained or paid out in dividends.
- Companies with outstanding debt often are restricted in the amount of dividends they can pay because of debt covenants and legal restrictions. Some institutions require that a company pay a dividend to be on their "approved" investment list. If a company funds capital expenditures by borrowing while paying earnings out in dividends, it will incur flotation costs on new debt issues.
- Using a stable dividend policy, a company tries to align its dividend growth rate to the company's long-term earnings growth rate. Dividends may increase even in years when earnings decline, and dividends will increase at a lower rate than earnings in boom years.
- A stable dividend policy can be represented by a gradual adjustment process in which the expected dividend is equal to last year's dividend per share plus [(Expected earnings × Target payout ratio – Previous dividend) × Adjustment factor].

- Using a constant dividend payout ratio policy, a company applies a target dividend payout ratio to current earnings; therefore, dividends are more volatile than with a stable dividend policy.
- Share repurchases, or buybacks, most often occur in the open market. Alternatively, tender offers occur at a fixed price or at a price range through a Dutch auction. Shareholders who do not tender increase their relative position in the company. Direct negotiations with major shareholders to get them to sell their positions are less common because they could destroy value for remaining stockholders.
- Share repurchases made with excess cash have the potential to increase earnings per share, whereas share repurchases made with borrowed funds can increase, decrease, or not affect earnings per share depending on the company's after-tax borrowing rate and earnings yield.
- A share repurchase is equivalent to the payment of a cash dividend of equal amount in its effect on total shareholders' wealth, all other things being equal.
- If the buyback market price per share is greater (less) than the book value per share, then the book value per share will decrease (increase).
- Companies can repurchase shares in lieu of increasing cash dividends. Share repurchases usually offer company management more flexibility than cash dividends by not establishing the expectation that a particular level of cash distribution will be maintained.
- Companies can pay regular cash dividends supplemented by share repurchases. In years of extraordinary increases in earnings, share repurchases can substitute for special cash dividends.
- On the one hand, share repurchases can signal that company officials think their shares are undervalued. On the other hand, share repurchases could send a negative signal that the company has few positive NPV opportunities.
- Analysts are interested in how safe a company's dividend is, specifically whether the company's earnings and, more importantly, its cash flow are sufficient to sustain the payment of the dividend.
- Early warning signs of whether a company can sustain its dividend include the dividend coverage ratio, the level of dividend yield, whether the company borrows to pay the dividend, and the company's past dividend record.

PRACTICE PROBLEMS

1. The payment of a 10% stock dividend by a company will result in an increase in that company's:
   A. current ratio.
   B. financial leverage.
   C. contributed capital.

2. If a company's common shares trade at very low prices, that company would be *most likely* to consider the use of a:
   A. stock split.
   B. stock dividend.
   C. reverse stock split.

3. In a recent presentation, Doug Pearce made two statements about dividends:

    Statement 1 "A stock dividend will increase share price on the ex-dividend date, all other things being equal."
    Statement 2 "One practical concern with a stock split is that it will reduce the company's price-to-earnings ratio."

    Are Pearce's two statements about the effects of the stock dividend and stock split correct?
    A. No for both statements.
    B. Yes for Statement 1, and no for Statement 2.
    C. No for Statement 1, and yes for Statement 2.

4. All other things being equal, the payment of an internally financed cash dividend is *most likely* to result in:
    A. a lower current ratio.
    B. a higher current ratio.
    C. the same current ratio.

The following information relates to questions 5-9

John Ladan is an analyst in the research department of an international securities firm. Ladan is currently analyzing Yeta Products, a publicly traded global consumer goods company located in the United States. Selected data for Yeta are presented in Exhibit 1.

EXHIBIT 1: Selected Financial Data for Yeta Products

Most Recent Fiscal Year		Current	
Pretax income	US$280 million	Shares outstanding	100 million
Net income after tax	US$182 million	Book value per share	US$25.60
Cash flow from operations	US$235 million	Share price	US$20.00
Capital expenditures	US$175 million		
Earnings per share	US$1.82		

Yeta currently does not pay a dividend, and the company operates with a target capital structure of 40% debt and 60% equity. However, on a recent conference call, Yeta's management indicated that they are considering four payout proposals:

Proposal #1: Issue a 10% stock dividend.
Proposal #2: Repurchase US$40 million in shares using surplus cash.
Proposal #3: Repurchase US$40 million in shares by borrowing US$40 million at an after-tax cost of borrowing of 8.50%.
Proposal #4: Initiate a regular cash dividend.

5. The implementation of Proposal #1 would generally lead to shareholders:
    A. having to pay tax on the dividend received.
    B. experiencing a decrease in the total cost basis of their shares.
    C. having the same proportionate ownership as before implementation.

6. If Yeta's management implemented Proposal #2 at the current share price shown in Exhibit 1, Yeta's book value per share after implementation would be *closest* to:
    A. US$25.20.
    B. US$25.71.
    C. US$26.12.

7. Based on Exhibit 1, if Yeta's management implemented Proposal #3 at the current share price, earnings per share would:
    A. decrease.
    B. remain unchanged.
    C. increase.

8. Based on Yeta's target capital structure, Proposal #4 will *most likely:*
    A. increase the default risk of Yeta's debt.
    B. increase the agency conflict between Yeta's shareholders and managers.
    C. decrease the agency conflict between Yeta's shareholders and bondholders.

9. The implementation of Proposal #4 would *most likely* signal to Ladan and other investors that future earnings growth can be expected to:
    A. decrease.
    B. remain unchanged.
    C. increase.

10. Match the phrases in Column A with the corresponding dividend theory in Column B. Note that you may use the answers in Column B more than once.

Column A	Column B
1. Bird in the hand	a) Dividend policy matters
2. Homemade dividends	b) Dividend policy is irrelevant
3. High tax rates on dividends	

11. Which of the following assumptions is *not* required for Miller and Modigliani's (MM) dividend theory?
    A. Shareholders have no transaction costs when buying and selling shares.
    B. There are no taxes.
    C. Investors prefer dividends over uncertain capital gains.

12. Sophie Chan owns 100,000 shares of PAT Company. PAT is selling for €40 per share, so Chan's investment is worth €4,000,000. Chan reinvests the gross amount of all dividends received to purchase additional shares. Assume that the clientele for PAT shares consists of tax-exempt investors. If PAT pays a €1.50 dividend, Chan's new share ownership after reinvesting dividends at the ex-dividend price is *most likely* to be closest to:
    A. 103,600.
    B. 103,750.
    C. 103,900.

13. Which of the following is *most likely* to signal negative information concerning a company?
   A. Share repurchase.
   B. Decrease in the quarterly dividend rate.
   C. A two-for-one stock split.

14. WL Corporation is located in a jurisdiction that has a 40% corporate tax rate on pretax income and a 30% personal tax rate on dividends. WL distributes all its after-tax income to shareholders. What is the effective tax rate on WL pretax income distributed in dividends?
   A. 42%.
   B. 58%.
   C. 70%.

15. Which of the following factors is *least likely* to be associated with a company having a low dividend payout ratio?
   A. High flotation costs on new equity issues.
   B. High tax rates on dividends.
   C. Low growth prospects.

16. The dividend policy of Berkshire Gardens Inc. can be represented by a gradual adjustment to a target dividend payout ratio. Last year Berkshire had earnings per share of US$3.00 and paid a dividend of US$0.60 a share. This year it estimates earnings per share will be US$4.00. Find its dividend per share for this year if it has a 25% target payout ratio and uses a five-year period to adjust its dividend.
   A. US$0.68.
   B. US$0.80.
   C. US$0.85.

17. Beta Corporation is a manufacturer of inflatable furniture. Which of the following scenarios best reflects a stable dividend policy for Beta?
   A. Maintaining a constant dividend payout ratio of 40–50%.
   B. Maintaining the dividend at US$1.00 a share for several years given no change in Beta's long-term prospects.
   C. Increasing the dividend 5% a year over several years to reflect the two years in which Beta recognized mark-to-market gains on derivatives positions.

18. A company has 1 million shares outstanding and earnings are £2 million. The company decides to use £10 million in surplus cash to repurchase shares in the open market. The company's shares are trading at £50 per share. If the company uses the entire £10 million of surplus cash to repurchase shares at the market price, the company's earnings per share will be *closest* to:
   A. £2.00.
   B. £2.30.
   C. £2.50.

19. Devon Ltd. common shares sell at US$40 a share, and their estimated price-to-earnings ratio (P/E) is 32. If Devon borrows funds to repurchase shares at its after-tax cost of debt of 5%, its EPS is *most likely* to:

A. increase.

B. decrease.

C. remain the same.

20. A company can borrow funds at an after-tax cost of 4.5%. The company's stock price is US$40 per share, earnings per share is US$2.00, and the company has 15 million shares outstanding. If the company borrows just enough to repurchase 2 million shares of stock at the prevailing market price, that company's earnings per share is *most likely* to:

A. increase.

B. decrease.

C. remain the same.

21. Crozet Corporation plans to borrow just enough money to repurchase 100,000 shares. The following information relates to the share repurchase:

Shares outstanding before buyback	3.1 million
Earnings per share before buyback	US$4.00
Share price at time of buyback	US$50
After-tax cost of borrowing	6%

Crozet's earnings per share after the buyback will be *closest* to:

A. US$4.03.

B. US$4.10.

C. US$4.23.

22. A company with 20 million shares outstanding decides to repurchase 2 million shares at the prevailing market price of €30 per share. At the time of the buyback, the company reports total assets of €850 million and total liabilities of €250 million. As a result of the buyback, that company's book value per share will *most likely*:

A. increase.

B. decrease.

C. remain the same.

23. An analyst gathered the following information about a company:

Number of shares outstanding	10 million
Earnings per share	US$2.00
P/E	20
Book value per share	US$30

If the company repurchases 1 million shares at the prevailing market price, the resulting book value per share will be *closest* to:

A. US$26.

B. US$27.

C. US$29.

24. If a company's objective is to support its stock price in the event of a market downturn, it would be advised to authorize:
    A. an open market share repurchase plan to be executed over the next five years.
    B. a tender offer share repurchase at a fixed price effective in 30 days.
    C. a Dutch auction tender offer effective in 30 days.

25. A company has positive free cash flow and is considering whether to use the entire amount of that free cash flow to pay a special cash dividend or to repurchase shares at the prevailing market price. Shareholders' wealth under the two options will be equivalent unless the:
    A. company's book value per share is less than the prevailing market price.
    B. company's book value per share is greater than the prevailing market price.
    C. tax consequences and/or information content for each alternative is different.

26. Assume that a company is based in a country that has no taxes on dividends or capital gains. The company is considering either paying a special dividend or repurchasing its own shares. Shareholders of the company would have:
    A. greater wealth if the company paid a special cash dividend.
    B. greater wealth if the company repurchased its shares.
    C. the same wealth under either a cash dividend or share repurchase program.

27. Investors may prefer companies that repurchase their shares instead of paying a cash dividend when:
    A. capital gains are taxed at lower rates than dividends.
    B. capital gains are taxed at the same rate as dividends.
    C. the company needs more equity to finance capital expenditures.

The following information relates to questions 28–29

Janet Wu is treasurer of Wilson Chemical Company, a manufacturer of specialty chemicals used in industrial manufacturing and increasingly in technology applications. Wilson Chemical is selling one of its older divisions for US$70 million cash. Wu is considering whether to recommend a special dividend of US$70 million or a repurchase of 2 million shares of Wilson common stock in the open market. She is reviewing some possible effects of the buyback with the company's financial analyst. Wilson has a long-term record of gradually increasing earnings and dividends.

28. Wilson's share buyback could be a signal that the company:
    A. is decreasing its financial leverage.
    B. views its shares as undervalued in the marketplace.
    C. has more investment opportunities than it could fund internally.

29. The most likely tax environment in which Wilson Chemical's shareholders would prefer that Wilson repurchase its shares (share buybacks) instead of paying dividends is one in which:
    A. the tax rate on capital gains and dividends is the same.
    B. capital gains tax rates are higher than dividend income tax rates.
    C. capital gains tax rates are lower than dividend income tax rates.

CHAPTER 10

BUSINESS MODELS & RISKS

LEARNING OUTCOMES

The candidate should be able to

- describe key features and types of business models
- describe expected relations between a company's external environment, business model, and financing needs
- explain and classify types of business and financial risks for a company

SUMMARY

- A business model describes how a business is organized to deliver value to its customers:
  - who its customers are,
  - how the business serves them,
  - key assets and suppliers, and
  - the supporting business logic.
- The firm's "value proposition" refers to the product or service attributes valued by a firm's target customer that lead those customers to prefer a firm's offering over those of its competitors, given relative pricing.
- Channel strategy may be a key element of a business model, and it addresses how the firm is reaching its customers.
- Pricing is often a key element of the business model. Pricing approaches are typically value or cost based.
- In addition to the value proposition, a business model should address the "value chain" and "how" the firm is structured to deliver that value.
- While many firms have conventional business models that are easily understood and described in simple terms, many business models are complex, specialized, or new.
- Digital technology has enabled significant business model innovation, often based on network effects.
- To understand the profitability of a business, the analyst should examine margins, break-even points, and "unit economics."
- Businesses have very different financing needs and risk profiles, depending on both external and firm-specific factors, which will determine the ability of the firm to raise capital.

PRACTICE PROBLEMS

1. Which of the following is *least likely* to be a key feature of a business model?
   A. Unit economics
   B. Channel strategy
   C. Financial forecasts
   D. Customer cost of ownership
   E. Target customer identification

2. When should an analyst expect a business model to employ premium pricing? When:
   A. the company is a price taker.
   B. the firm is small and returns are highly scale sensitive.
   C. significant differentiation is possible in the product category.
   D. the firm is a market leader and demand is very price sensitive.

3. Which is the *most accurate* statement about a platform business?
   A. A platform business is based on network effects.
   B. A platform business can be a non-technology business.
   C. Value creation for customers for a platform business occurs externally.
   D. It can be difficult to attract users in the beginning to a platform business.
   E. All of the above

4. Which of the following businesses is *least likely* to have network effects?
   A. A stock exchange
   B. A telephone company
   C. A classified advertising website
   D. A price comparison website for travel airfares
   E. A resume preparation service for online job seekers

5. A flower shop has preferred supplier arrangements with an answering service, to take orders after hours, and a bicycle delivery service, to ensure that it can make deliveries quickly, reliably, and at a reasonable cost. Which of the following statements is *most accurate* for the flower shop?
   A. The answering service is part of its supply chain.
   B. The bicycle delivery service is part of its value chain.
   C. The bicycle delivery service is part of its supply chain.
   D. The bicycle delivery service is not a part of the value proposition for the flower shop.

6. Which of the following is the *closest* example of a one-sided network?
   A. An online employment website
   B. A dating website for men and women
   C. A social network for model train collectors
   D. A website for home improvement contractors

7. Which of the following statements is not representative of unit costs?
   A. Unit costs generally exclude labor costs.
   B. Business models generally consider unit costs.
   C. Unit costs are used to calculate break-even points.
   D. If a lemonade stand uses 5 cents worth of lemons, 2 cents worth of sugar, and a cup costing 3 cents for each glass of lemonade, it has a unit cost of 10 cents.

8. Which of the following companies would *most likely* have a high level of macro risk?
   A. A coffee plantation in Brazil
   B. A Swedish mining equipment manufacturer
   C. A call center outsourcing business based in India

9. Which of the following is *most likely* to have a high level of industry risk?
   A. Toll road
   B. Pest control services company
   C. Oil well drilling service company

10. For a newly launched clothing company in Japan that uses offshore production in Malaysia, classify each of the following impacts:

1. Demand falls gradually due to a declining population	A. Company-specific risk
2. Consumer tastes shift to favor locally manufactured apparel	B. Macro risk
3. The company faces uncertainty about future demand as it hires a new chief designer and makes changes to its top-selling products	C. Industry risk

11. Which of the following is an example of significant execution risk?
    A. A manufacturer replaces aging factory machinery with similar but more efficient equipment.
    B. A marketer of high-fashion pet accessories tests the market to see if there is demand for glamourous dog harnesses made with faux fur.
    C. A company with consistent operating margins of about 5% with stable market share of 5% for swimming pool chemicals plans to double its margins and triple its market share over the next five years.

12. Which of the following is *most likely* to increase a business's operating leverage?
    A. Reducing prices
    B. Borrowing rather than issuing equity
    C. Using casual labor rather than a salaried work force

13. Which of the following is *most likely* to increase financial leverage?
    A. Cutting prices
    B. Replacing short-term debt with long-term debt
    C. Entering a sale-leaseback transaction for the company's head office building

CHAPTER 11

THE FIRM AND MARKET STRUCTURES

LEARNING OUTCOMES

The candidate should be able to:

- describe characteristics of perfect competition, monopolistic competition, oligopoly, and pure monopoly
- explain relationships between price, marginal revenue, marginal cost, economic profit, and the elasticity of demand under each market structure
- describe a firm's supply function under each market structure
- describe and determine the optimal price and output for firms under each market structure
- describe pricing strategy under each market structure
- explain factors affecting long-run equilibrium under each market structure
- describe the use and limitations of concentration measures in identifying market structure
- identify the type of market structure within which a firm operates

SUMMARY

In this chapter, we have surveyed how economists classify market structures. We have analyzed the distinctions between the different structures that are important for understanding demand and supply relations, optimal price and output, and the factors affecting long-run profitability. We also provided guidelines for identifying market structure in practice. Among our conclusions are the following:

- Economic market structures can be grouped into four categories: perfect competition, monopolistic competition, oligopoly, and monopoly.
- The categories differ because of the following characteristics: The number of producers is many in perfect and monopolistic competition, few in oligopoly, and one in monopoly. The degree of product differentiation, the pricing power of the producer, the barriers to entry of new producers, and the level of non-price competition (e.g., advertising) are all low in perfect competition, moderate in monopolistic competition, high in oligopoly, and generally highest in monopoly.

- A financial analyst must understand the characteristics of market structures in order to better forecast a firm's future profit stream.
- The optimal marginal revenue equals marginal cost. However, only in perfect competition does the marginal revenue equal price. In the remaining structures, price generally exceeds marginal revenue because a firm can sell more units only by reducing the per unit price.
- The quantity sold is highest in perfect competition. The price in perfect competition is usually lowest, but this depends on factors such as demand elasticity and increasing returns to scale (which may reduce the producer's marginal cost). Monopolists, oligopolists, and producers in monopolistic competition attempt to differentiate their products so that they can charge higher prices.
- Typically, monopolists sell a smaller quantity at a higher price. Investors may benefit from being shareholders of monopolistic firms that have large margins and substantial positive cash flows.
- Competitive firms do not earn economic profit. There will be a market compensation for the rental of capital and of management services, but the lack of pricing power implies that there will be no extra margins.
- While in the short run firms in any market structure can have economic profits, the more competitive a market is and the lower the barriers to entry, the faster the extra profits will fade. In the long run, new entrants shrink margins and push the least efficient firms out of the market.
- Oligopoly is characterized by the importance of strategic behavior. Firms can change the price, quantity, quality, and advertisement of the product to gain an advantage over their competitors. Several types of equilibrium (e.g., Nash, Cournot, kinked demand curve) may occur that affect the likelihood of each of the incumbents (and potential entrants in the long run) having economic profits. Price wars may be started to force weaker competitors to abandon the market.
- Measuring market power is complicated. Ideally, econometric estimates of the elasticity of demand and supply should be computed. However, because of the lack of reliable data and the fact that elasticity changes over time (so that past data may not apply to the current situation), regulators and economists often use simpler measures. The concentration ratio is simple, but the HHI, with little more computation required, often produces a better figure for decision making.

PRACTICE PROBLEMS

1. A market structure characterized by many sellers with each having some pricing power and product differentiation is *best* described as:
   A. oligopoly.
   B. perfect competition.
   C. monopolistic competition.

2. A market structure with relatively few sellers of a homogeneous or standardized product is *best* described as:
   A. oligopoly.
   B. monopoly.
   C. perfect competition.

3. The demand schedule in a perfectly competitive market is given by $P = 93 - 1.5Q$ (for $Q \leq 62$) and the long-run cost structure of each company is:

    Total cost: $256 + 2Q + 4Q^2$

    Average cost: $256/Q + 2 + 4Q$

    Marginal cost: $2 + 8Q$

    New companies will enter the market at any price greater than:
    A. 8.
    B. 66.
    C. 81.

4. If companies earn economic profits in a perfectly competitive market, over the long run the supply curve will *most likely*:
    A. shift to the left.
    B. shift to the right.
    C. remain unchanged.

5. A company doing business in a monopolistically competitive market will *most likely* maximize profits when its output quantity is set such that:
    A. average cost is minimized.
    B. marginal revenue equals average cost.
    C. marginal revenue equals marginal cost.

6. Oligopolistic pricing strategy *most likely* results in a demand curve that is:
    A. kinked.
    B. vertical.
    C. horizontal.

7. Collusion is *less likely* in a market when:
    A. the product is homogeneous.
    B. companies have similar market shares.
    C. the cost structures of companies are similar.

8. In an industry comprised of three companies, which are small-scale manufacturers of an easily replicable product unprotected by brand recognition or patents, the *most* representative model of company behavior is:
    A. oligopoly.
    B. perfect competition.
    C. monopolistic competition.

9. Deep River Manufacturing is one of many companies in an industry that makes a food product. Deep River units are identical up to the point they are labeled. Deep River produces its labeled brand, which sells for $2.20 per unit, and "house brands" for seven different grocery chains which sell for $2.00 per unit. Each grocery chain sells both the Deep River brand and its house brand. The *best* characterization of Deep River's market is:
    A. oligopoly.
    B. perfect competition.
    C. monopolistic competition.

10. SigmaSoft and ThetaTech are the dominant makers of computer system software. The market has two components: a large mass-market component in which demand is price sensitive, and a smaller performance-oriented component in which demand is much less price sensitive. SigmaSoft's product is considered to be technically superior. Each company can choose one of two strategies:

- *Open architecture (Open):* Mass market focus allowing other software venders to develop products for its platform.
- *Proprietary (Prop):* Allow only its own software applications to run on its platform.

Depending upon the strategy each company selects, their profits would be:

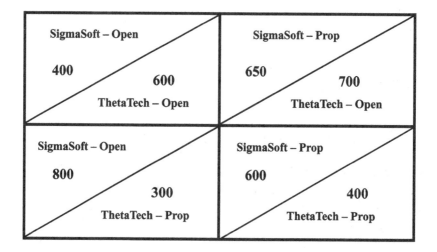

The Nash equilibrium for these companies is:
A. proprietary for SigmaSoft and proprietary for ThetaTech.
B. open architecture for SigmaSoft and proprietary for ThetaTech.
C. proprietary for SigmaSoft and open architecture for ThetaTech.

11. Companies *most likely* have a well-defined supply function when the market structure is:
A. oligopoly.
B. perfect competition.
C. monopolistic competition.

12. Aquarius, Inc. is the dominant company and the price leader in its market. One of the other companies in the market attempts to gain market share by undercutting the price set by Aquarius. The market share of Aquarius will *most likely*:
A. increase.
B. decrease.
C. stay the same.

13. Over time, the market share of the dominant company in an oligopolistic market will *most likely*:
    A. increase.
    B. decrease.
    C. remain the same.

14. Market competitors are *least likely* to use advertising as a tool of differentiation in an industry structure identified as:
    A. monopoly.
    B. perfect competition.
    C. monopolistic competition.

15. Upsilon Natural Gas, Inc. is a monopoly enjoying very high barriers to entry. Its marginal cost is $40 and its average cost is $70. A recent market study has determined the price elasticity of demand is 1.5. The company will *most likely* set its price at:
    A. $40.
    B. $70.
    C. $120.

16. A government entity that regulates an authorized monopoly will *most likely* base regulated prices on:
    A. marginal cost.
    B. long run average cost.
    C. first degree price discrimination.

17. An analyst gathers the following market share data for an industry:

Company	Sales (in millions of €)
ABC	300
Brown	250
Coral	200
Delta	150
Erie	100
All others	50

The industry's four-company concentration ratio is *closest* to:
A. 71%.
B. 86%.
C. 95%.

18. An analyst gathered the following market share data for an industry comprised of five companies:

Company	Market Share (%)
Zeta	35
Yusef	25
Xenon	20
Waters	10
Vlastos	10

The industry's three-firm Herfindahl–Hirschmann Index is *closest* to:
A. 0.185.
B. 0.225.
C. 0.235.

19. One disadvantage of the Herfindahl–Hirschmann Index is that the index:
A. is difficult to compute.
B. fails to reflect low barriers to entry.
C. fails to reflect the effect of mergers in the industry.

CHAPTER 12

INTRODUCTION TO INDUSTRY AND COMPANY ANALYSIS

LEARNING OUTCOMES

The candidate should be able to:

- explain uses of industry analysis and the relation of industry analysis to company analysis
- compare methods by which companies can be grouped
- explain the factors that affect the sensitivity of a company to the business cycle and the uses and limitations of industry and company descriptors such as "growth," "defensive," and "cyclical"
- describe current industry classification systems, and identify how a company should be classified, given a description of its activities and the classification system
- explain how a company's industry classification can be used to identify a potential "peer group" for equity valuation
- describe the elements that need to be covered in a thorough industry analysis
- describe the principles of strategic analysis of an industry
- explain the effects of barriers to entry, industry concentration, industry capacity, and market share stability on pricing power and price competition
- describe industry life-cycle models, classify an industry as to life-cycle stage, and describe limitations of the life-cycle concept in forecasting industry performance
- describe macroeconomic, technological, demographic, governmental, social, and environmental influences on industry growth, profitability, and risk
- compare characteristics of representative industries from the various economic sectors
- describe the elements that should be covered in a thorough company analysis

SUMMARY

In this chapter, we have provided an overview of industry analysis and illustrated approaches that are widely used by analysts to examine an industry.

- Company analysis and industry analysis are closely interrelated. Company and industry analysis together can provide insight into sources of industry revenue growth and competitors' market shares and thus the future of an individual company's top-line growth and bottom-line profitability.
- Industry analysis is useful for
  - understanding a company's business and business environment,
  - identifying active equity investment opportunities,
  - formulating an industry or sector rotation strategy, and
  - portfolio performance attribution.

- The three main approaches to classifying companies are
  - products and/or services supplied,
  - business-cycle sensitivities, and
  - statistical similarities.

- A cyclical company is one whose profits are strongly correlated with the strength of the overall economy.
- A non-cyclical company is one whose performance is largely independent of the business cycle.
- Commercial industry classification systems include
  - The Global Industry Classification Standard (GICS)
  - The Industry Classification Benchmark (ICB)

- A limitation of current classification systems is that the narrowest classification unit assigned to a company generally cannot be assumed to constitute its peer group for the purposes of detailed fundamental comparisons or valuation.
- A peer group is a group of companies engaged in similar business activities whose economics and valuation are influenced by closely related factors.
- The steps in constructing a preliminary list of peer companies are as follows:
  - Examine commercial classification systems if available. These systems often provide a useful starting point for identifying companies operating in the same industry.
  - Review the subject company's annual report for a discussion of the competitive environment. Companies frequently cite specific competitors.
  - Review competitors' annual reports to identify other potential comparables.
  - Review industry trade publications to identify additional peer companies.
  - Confirm that each comparable or peer company derives a significant portion of its revenue and operating profit from a business activity similar to that of the subject company.

- Not all industries are created equal. Some are highly competitive, with many companies struggling to earn returns in excess of their cost of capital, and other industries have attractive characteristics that enable a majority of industry participants to generate healthy profits.
- Differing competitive environments are determined by the structural attributes of the industry. For this important reason, industry analysis is a vital complement to company analysis. The analyst needs to understand the context in which a company operates to fully understand the opportunities and threats that a company faces.
- The framework for strategic analysis known as "Porter's five forces" can provide a useful starting point. Porter maintained that the profitability of companies in an industry is

determined by five forces: (1) the threat of new entrants, which, in turn, is determined by economies of scale, brand loyalty, absolute cost advantages, customer switching costs, and government regulation; (2) the bargaining power of suppliers, which is a function of the feasibility of product substitution, the concentration of the buyer and supplier groups, and switching costs and entry costs in each case; (3) the bargaining power of buyers, which is a function of switching costs among customers and the ability of customers to produce their own product; (4) the threat of substitutes; and (5) the intensity of rivalry among existing competitors, which, in turn, is a function of industry competitive structure, demand conditions, cost conditions, and the height of exit barriers.

- The concept of barriers to entry refers to the ease with which new competitors can challenge incumbents and can be an important factor in determining the competitive environment of an industry. If new competitors can easily enter the industry, the industry is likely to be highly competitive because incumbents that attempt to raise prices will be undercut by newcomers. As a result, industries with low barriers to entry tend to have low pricing power. Conversely, if incumbents are protected by barriers to entry, they may enjoy a more benign competitive environment that gives them greater pricing power over their customers because they do not have to worry about being undercut by startups.

- Industry concentration is often, although not always, a sign that an industry may have pricing power and rational competition. Industry fragmentation is a much stronger signal, however, that the industry is competitive and pricing power is limited.

- The effect of industry capacity on pricing is clear: Tight capacity gives participants more pricing power because demand for products or services exceeds supply; overcapacity leads to price cutting and a highly competitive environment as excess supply chases demand. The analyst should think about not only current capacity conditions but also future changes in capacity levels—how long it takes for supply and demand to come into balance and what effect that process has on industry pricing power and returns.

- Examining the market share stability of an industry over time is similar to thinking about barriers to entry and the frequency with which new players enter an industry. Stable market shares typically indicate less competitive industries, whereas unstable market shares often indicate highly competitive industries with limited pricing power.

- An industry's position in its life cycle often has a large impact on its competitive dynamics, so it is important to keep this positioning in mind when performing strategic analysis of an industry. Industries, like individual companies, tend to evolve over time and usually experience significant changes in the rate of growth and levels of profitability along the way. Just as an investment in an individual company requires careful monitoring, industry analysis is a continuous process that must be repeated over time to identify changes that may be occurring.

- A useful framework for analyzing the evolution of an industry is an industry life-cycle model, which identifies the sequential stages that an industry typically goes through. The five stages of an industry life cycle according to the Hill and Jones model are
  - embryonic,
  - growth,
  - shakeout,
  - mature, and
  - decline.

- Price competition and thinking like a customer are important factors that are often overlooked when analyzing an industry. Whatever factors most influence customer purchasing decisions are also likely to be the focus of competitive rivalry in the industry. Broadly, industries for which price is a large factor in customer purchase decisions tend to be more competitive than industries in which customers value other attributes more highly.
- External influences on industry growth, profitability, and risk include
  - technology,
  - demographics,
  - government,
  - social factors, and
  - environmental factors.

- Company analysis takes place after the analyst has gained an understanding of the company's external environment and includes answering questions about how the company will respond to the threats and opportunities presented by the external environment. This intended response is the individual company's competitive strategy. The analyst should seek to determine whether the strategy is primarily defensive or offensive in its nature and how the company intends to implement it.
- Porter identified two chief competitive strategies:
  - A low-cost strategy (cost leadership) is one in which companies strive to become the low-cost producers and to gain market share by offering their products and services at lower prices than their competition while still making a profit margin sufficient to generate a superior rate of return based on the higher revenues achieved.
  - A product/service differentiation strategy is one in which companies attempt to establish themselves as the suppliers or producers of products and services that are unique either in quality, type, or means of distribution. To be successful, the companies' price premiums must be above their costs of differentiation and the differentiation must be appealing to customers and sustainable over time.

- A checklist for company analysis includes a thorough investigation of
  - the corporate profile,
  - industry characteristics,
  - demand for products/services,
  - supply of products/services,
  - pricing,
  - financial ratios, and
  - sustainability metrics.

- Spreadsheet modeling of financial statements to analyze and forecast revenues, operating and net income, and cash flows is one of the most widely used tools in company analysis. Spreadsheet modeling can be used to quantify the effects of the changes in certain swing factors on the various financial statements. The analyst should be aware that the output of the model will depend significantly on the assumptions that are made.

PRACTICE PROBLEMS

1. Which of the following is *least likely* to involve industry analysis?
   A. Sector rotation strategy
   B. Top-down fundamental investing
   C. Tactical asset allocation strategy

2. A sector rotation strategy involves investing in a sector by:
   A. making regular investments in it.
   B. investing in a pre-selected group of sectors on a rotating basis.
   C. timing investment to take advantage of business-cycle conditions.

3. Which of the following information about a company would *most likely* depend on an industry analysis? The company's:
   A. treatment of long-lived assets on its financial statements.
   B. competitive environment.
   C. trends in corporate expenses.

4. Which of the following is *not* a limitation of the cyclical/non-cyclical descriptive approach to classifying companies?
   A. A cyclical company may have a growth component in it.
   B. Business-cycle sensitivity is a discrete phenomenon rather than a continuous spectrum.
   C. A global company can experience economic expansion in one part of the world while experiencing recession in another part.

5. A cyclical company is *most likely* to:
   A. have low operating leverage.
   B. sell relatively inexpensive products.
   C. experience wider-than-average fluctuations in demand.

6. A company that is sensitive to the business cycle would *most likely*:
   A. not have growth opportunities.
   B. experience below-average fluctuation in demand.
   C. sell products that customers can purchase at a later date if necessary.

7. Which of the following factors would *most likely* be a limitation of applying business-cycle analysis to global industry analysis?
   A. Some industries are relatively insensitive to the business cycle.
   B. Correlations of security returns between different world markets are relatively low.
   C. One region or country of the world may experience recession while another region experiences expansion.

8. In which sector would a manufacturer of personal care products be classified?
   A. Health care
   B. Consumer staples
   C. Consumer discretionary

9. An automobile manufacturer is *most likely* classified in which of the following industry sectors?
   A. Consumer staples
   B. Industrial durables
   C. Consumer discretionary

10. Which of the following statements about commercial and government industry classification systems is *most* accurate?
    A. Many commercial classification systems include private for-profit companies.
    B. Both commercial and government classification systems exclude not-for-profit companies.
    C. Commercial classification systems are generally updated more frequently than government classification systems.

11. Which of the following statements about peer groups is *most* accurate?
    A. Constructing a peer group for a company follows a standardized process.
    B. Commercial industry classification systems often provide a starting point for constructing a peer group.
    C. A peer group is generally composed of all the companies in the most narrowly defined category used by the commercial industry classification system.

12. With regard to forming a company's peer group, which of the following statements is *not* correct?
    A. Comments from the management of the company about competitors are generally not used when selecting the peer group.
    B. The higher the proportion of revenue and operating profit of the peer company derived from business activities similar to those of the subject company, the more meaningful the comparison.
    C. Comparing the company's performance measures with those for a potential peer-group company is of limited value when the companies are exposed to different stages of the business cycle.

13. When selecting companies for inclusion in a peer group, a company operating in three different business segments would:
    A. be in only one peer group.
    B. possibly be in more than one peer group.
    C. not be included in any peer group.

14. An industry that *most likely* has both high barriers to entry and high barriers to exit is the:
    A. restaurant industry.
    B. advertising industry.
    C. automobile industry.

15. Which factor is *most likely* associated with stable market share?
    A. Low switching costs
    B. Low barriers to entry
    C. Slow pace of product innovation

16. Which of the following companies *most likely* has the greatest ability to quickly increase its capacity to offer goods or services?

    A. A restaurant

    B. A steel producer

    C. An insurance company

17. Which of the following life-cycle phases is typically characterized by high prices?

    A. Mature

    B. Growth

    C. Embryonic

18. In which of the following life-cycle phases are price wars *most likely* to be absent?

    A. Mature

    B. Decline

    C. Growth

19. When graphically depicting the life-cycle model for an industry as a curve, the variables on the axes are:

    A. price and time.

    B. demand and time.

    C. demand and stage of the life cycle.

20. Industry consolidation and high barriers to entry *most likely* characterize which life-cycle stage?

    A. Mature

    B. Growth

    C. Embryonic

21. Which of the following is *most likely* a characteristic of a concentrated industry?

    A. Infrequent, tacit coordination

    B. Difficulty in monitoring other industry members

    C. Industry members attempting to avoid competition on price

22. Which of the following industry characteristics is generally *least likely* to produce high returns on capital?

    A. High barriers to entry

    B. High degree of concentration

    C. Short lead time to build new plants

23. An industry with high barriers to entry and weak pricing power *most likely* has:

    A. high barriers to exit.

    B. stable market shares.

    C. significant numbers of issued patents.

24. Economic value is created for an industry's shareholders when the industry earns a return:

    A. below the cost of capital.

    B. equal to the cost of capital.

    C. above the cost of capital.

25. Which of the following industries is *most likely* to be characterized as concentrated with strong pricing power?

    A. Asset management

    B. Alcoholic beverages

    C. Household and personal products

26. A population that is rapidly aging would *most likely* cause the growth rate of the industry producing eyeglasses and contact lenses to:
    A. decrease.
    B. increase.
    C. not change.

27. If over a long period of time a country's average level of educational accomplishment increases, this development would *most likely* lead to the country's amount of income spent on consumer discretionary goods to:
    A. decrease.
    B. increase.
    C. not change.

28. If the technology for an industry involves high fixed capital investment, then one way to seek higher profit growth is by pursuing:
    A. economies of scale.
    B. diseconomies of scale.
    C. removal of features that differentiate the product or service provided.

29. With respect to competitive strategy, a company with a successful cost leadership strategy is *most likely* characterized by:
    A. a low cost of capital.
    B. reduced market share.
    C. the ability to offer products at higher prices than those of its competitors.

30. When conducting a company analysis, the analysis of demand for a company's product is *least likely* to consider the:
    A. company's cost structure.
    B. motivations of the customer base.
    C. product's differentiating characteristics.

31. Which of the following statements about company analysis is *most* accurate?
    A. The complexity of spreadsheet modeling ensures precise forecasts of financial statements.
    B. The interpretation of financial ratios should focus on comparing the company's results over time but not with competitors.
    C. The corporate profile would include a description of the company's business, investment activities, governance, and strengths and weaknesses.

CHAPTER 13

FINANCIAL STATEMENT MODELING

LEARNING OUTCOMES

The candidate should be able to:

- compare top-down, bottom-up, and hybrid approaches for developing inputs to equity valuation models
- compare "growth relative to GDP growth" and "market growth and market share" approaches to forecasting revenue
- evaluate whether economies of scale are present in an industry by analyzing operating margins and sales levels
- demonstrate methods to forecast the following costs: cost of goods sold, selling general and administrative costs, financing costs, and income taxes
- demonstrate methods to forecast non-operating items, financing costs, and income taxes
- describe approaches to balance sheet modeling
- demonstrate the development of a sales-based pro forma company model
- explain how behavioral factors affect analyst forecasts and recommend remedial actions for analyst biases
- explain how competitive factors affect prices and costs
- evaluate the competitive position of a company based on a Porter's five forces analysis
- explain how to forecast industry and company sales and costs when they are subject to price inflation or deflation
- evaluate the effects of technological developments on demand, selling prices, costs, and margins
- explain considerations in the choice of an explicit forecast horizon
- explain an analyst's choices in developing projections beyond the short-term forecast horizon

SUMMARY

Industry and company analysis are essential tools of fundamental analysis. The key points made include the following:

- Analysts can use a top-down, bottom-up, or hybrid approach to forecasting income and expenses. Top-down approaches usually begin at the level of the overall economy.

Bottom-up approaches begin at the level of the individual company or unit within the company (e.g., business segment). Time-series approaches are considered bottom-up, although time-series analysis can be a tool used in top-down approaches. Hybrid approaches include elements of top-down and bottom-up approaches.

- In a "growth relative to GDP growth" approach to forecasting revenue, the analyst forecasts the growth rate of nominal gross domestic product and industry and company growth relative to GDP growth.
- In a "market growth and market share" approach to forecasting revenue, the analyst combines forecasts of growth in particular markets with forecasts of a company's market share in the individual markets.
- Operating margins that are positively correlated with sales provide evidence of economies of scale in an industry.
- Some balance sheet line items, such as retained earnings, flow directly from the income statement, whereas accounts receivable, accounts payable, and inventory are very closely linked to income statement projections.
- A common way to model working capital accounts is to use efficiency ratios.
- Return on invested capital (ROIC), defined as net operating profit less adjusted taxes divided by the difference between operating assets and operating liabilities, is an after-tax measure of the profitability of investing in a company. High and persistent levels of ROIC are often associated with having a competitive advantage.
- Competitive factors affect a company's ability to negotiate lower input prices with suppliers and to raise prices for products and services. Porter's five forces framework can be used as a basis for identifying such factors.
- Inflation (deflation) affects pricing strategy depending on industry structure, competitive forces, and the nature of consumer demand.
- When a technological development results in a new product that threatens to cannibalize demand for an existing product, a unit forecast for the new product combined with an expected cannibalization factor can be used to estimate the impact on future demand for the existing product.
- Factors influencing the choice of the explicit forecast horizon include the projected holding period, an investor's average portfolio turnover, cyclicality of an industry, company-specific factors, and employer preferences.
- Key behavioral biases that influence analyst forecasts are overconfidence, illusion of control conservatism, representativeness, and confirmation bias.

PRACTICE PROBLEMS

The following information relates to questions 1–7

Angela Green, an investment manager at Horizon Investments, intends to hire a new investment analyst. After conducting initial interviews, Green has narrowed the pool to three candidates. She plans to conduct second interviews to further assess the candidates' knowledge of industry and company analysis.

Prior to the second interviews, Green asks the candidates to analyze Chrome Network Systems, a company that manufactures internet networking products. Each candidate is provided Chrome's financial information presented in Exhibit 1.

Exhibit 1: Chrome Network Systems Selected Financial Information ($ millions)

	Year-End		
	2017	2018	2019
Net sales	46.8	50.5	53.9
Cost of sales	18.2	18.4	18.8
Gross profit	28.6	32.1	35.1
SG&A expenses	19.3	22.5	25.1
Operating income	9.3	9.6	10.0
Interest expense	0.5	0.7	0.6
Income before provision for income tax	8.8	8.9	9.4
Provision for income taxes	2.8	2.8	3.1
Net income	6.0	6.1	6.3

Green asks each candidate to forecast the 2020 income statement for Chrome and to outline the key assumptions used in their analysis. The job candidates are told to include Horizon's economic outlook for 2020 in their analysis, which assumes nominal GDP growth of 3.6%, based on expectations of real GDP growth of 1.6% and inflation of 2.0%.

Green receives the models from each of the candidates and schedules second interviews. To prepare for the interviews, Green compiles a summary of the candidates' key assumptions in Exhibit 2.

Exhibit 2: Summary of Key Assumptions Used in Candidates' Models

Metric	Candidate A	Candidate B	Candidate C
Net sales	Net sales will grow at the average annual growth rate in net sales over the 2017–19 time period.	Industry sales will grow at the same rate as nominal GDP, but Chrome will have a 2 percentage point decline in market share.	Net sales will grow 50 bps slower than nominal GDP.
Cost of sales	The 2020 gross margin will be the same as the average annual gross margin over the 2017–19 time period.	The 2020 gross margin will decline as costs increase by expected inflation.	The 2020 gross margin will increase by 20 bps from 2019.
SG&A expenses	The 2020 SG&A/net sales ratio will be the same as the average ratio over the 2017–19 time period.	The 2020 SG&A will grow at the rate of inflation.	The 2020 SG&A/net sales ratio will be the same as the 2019 ratio.
Interest expense	The 2020 interest expense assumes the effective interest rate will be the same as the 2019 rate.	The 2020 interest expense will be the same as the 2019 interest expense.	The 2020 interest expense will be the same as the average expense over the 2017–19 time period.
Income taxes	The 2020 effective tax rate will be the same as the 2019 rate.	The 2020 effective tax rate will equal the blended statutory rate of 30%.	The 2020 effective tax rate will be the same as the average effective tax rate over the 2017–19 time period.

1. Based on Exhibit 1, which of the following provides the strongest evidence that Chrome displays economies of scale?
    A. Increasing net sales
    B. Profit margins that are increasing with net sales
    C. Gross profit margins that are increasing with net sales

2. Based on Exhibit 2, the job candidate *most likely* using a bottom-up approach to model net sales is:
    A. Candidate A
    B. Candidate B
    C. Candidate C

3. Based on Exhibit 2, the modeling approach used by Candidate B to project future net sales is *most accurately* classified as a:
    A. hybrid approach.
    B. top-down approach.
    C. bottom-up approach.

4. Based on Exhibits 1 and 2, Candidate C's forecast for cost of sales in 2020 is *closest* to:
    A. USD18.3 million.
    B. USD18.9 million.
    C. USD19.3 million.

5. Based on Exhibits 1 and 2, Candidate A's forecast for SG&A expenses in 2020 is *closest* to:
    A. USD23.8 million.
    B. USD25.5 million.
    C. USD27.4 million.

6. Based on Exhibit 2, forecasted interest expense will reflect changes in Chrome's debt level under the forecast assumptions used by:
    A. Candidate A.
    B. Candidate B.
    C. Candidate C.

7. Candidate B asks Green if she had additional information on Horizon's industry peers and competitors, to put the profitability estimates in a richer context. By asking for this additional information for their analysis, Candidate B is seeking to mitigate which behavioral bias?
    A. Illusion of control
    B. Base rate neglect
    C. Conservatism

The following information relates to questions 8–14

Nigel French, an analyst at Taurus Investment Management, is analyzing Archway Technologies, a manufacturer of luxury electronic auto equipment, at the request of his supervisor, Lukas Wright. French is asked to evaluate Archway's profitability over the past five years relative to its two main competitors, which are located in different countries with significantly different tax structures.

French begins by assessing Archway's competitive position within the luxury electronic auto equipment industry using Porter's five forces framework. A summary of French's industry analysis is presented in Exhibit 1.

Exhibit 1: Analysis of Luxury Electronic Auto Equipment Industry Using Porter's Five Forces Framework

Force	Factors to Consider
Threat of substitutes	Customer switching costs are high
Rivalry	Archway holds 60% of world market share; each of its two main competitors holds 15%
Bargaining power of suppliers	Primary inputs are considered basic commodities, and there are a large number of suppliers
Bargaining power of buyers	Luxury electronic auto equipment is very specialized (non-standardized)
Threat of new entrants	High fixed costs to enter industry

French notes that for the year just ended (2019), Archway's COGS was 30% of sales. To forecast Archway's income statement for 2020, French assumes that all companies in the industry will experience an inflation rate of 8% on the COGS. Exhibit 2 shows French's forecasts relating to Archway's price and volume changes.

Exhibit 2: Archway's 2020 Forecasted Price and Volume Changes

Average price increase per unit	5.00%
Volume growth	–3.00%

After putting together income statement projections for Archway, French forecasts Archway's balance sheet items. He uses Archway's historical efficiency ratios to forecast the company's working capital accounts.

Based on his financial forecast for Archway, French estimates a terminal value using a valuation multiple based on the company's average price-to-earnings multiple (P/E) over the past five years. Wright discusses with French how the terminal value estimate is sensitive to key assumptions about the company's future prospects. Wright asks French:

"What change in the calculation of the terminal value would you make if a technological development that would adversely affect Archway was forecast to occur sometime beyond your financial forecast horizon?"

8. Which profitability metric should French use to assess Archway's five-year historic performance relative to its competitors?
    A. Current ratio
    B. Operating margin
    C. Return on invested capital

9. Based on the current competitive landscape presented in Exhibit 1, French should conclude that Archway's ability to:
    A. pass along price increases is high.
    B. demand lower input prices from suppliers is low.
    C. generate above-average returns on invested capital is low.

10. Based on the current competitive landscape presented in Exhibit 1, Archway's operating profit margins over the forecast horizon are *least likely* to:
    A. decrease.
    B. remain constant.
    C. increase.

11. Based on Exhibit 2, Archway's forecasted gross profit margin for 2020 is *closest* to:
    A. 62.7%.
    B. 67.0%.
    C. 69.1%.

12. French's approach to forecasting Archway's working capital accounts would be *most likely* classified as a:
    A. hybrid approach.
    B. top-down approach.
    C. bottom-up approach.

13. The *most appropriate* response to Wright's question about the technological development is to:
    A. increase the required return.
    B. decrease the price-to-earnings multiple.
    C. decrease the perpetual growth rate.

14. If the luxury electronic auto equipment industry is subject to rapid technological changes and market share shifts, how should French best adapt his approach to modeling?
    A. Examine base rates
    B. Speak to analysts who hold diverse opinions on the stock
    C. Forecast multiple scenarios

The following information relates to questions 15–21

Gertrude Fromm is a transportation sector analyst at Tucana Investments. She is conducting an analysis of Omikroon, N.V., a (hypothetical) European engineering company that manufactures and sells scooters and commercial trucks.

Omikroon's petrol scooter division is the market leader in its sector and has two competitors. Omikroon's petrol scooters have a strong brand name and a well-established distribution network. Given the strong branding established by the market leaders, the cost of entering the industry is high. But Fromm anticipates that small, inexpensive, imported petrol-fueled motorcycles could become substitutes for Omikroon's petrol scooters.

Fromm uses ROIC as the metric to assess Omikroon's performance.

Omikroon has just introduced the first electric scooter to the market at year-end 2019. The company's expectations are as follows:

- Competing electric scooters will reach the market in 2021.
- Electric scooters will not be a substitute for petrol scooters.
- The important research costs in 2020 and 2021 will lead to more efficient electric scooters.

Fromm decides to use a five-year forecast horizon for Omikroon after considering the following factors:

Factor 1 The annual portfolio turnover at Tucana Investments is 30%.
Factor 2 The electronic scooter industry is expected to grow rapidly over the next 10 years.
Factor 3 Omikroon has announced it would acquire a light truck manufacturer that will be fully integrated into its truck division by 2021 and will add 2% to the company's total revenues.

Fromm uses the base case forecast for 2020 shown in Exhibit 1 to perform the following sensitivity analysis:

- The price of an imported specialty metal used for engine parts increases by 20%.
- This metal constitutes 4% of Omikroon's cost of sales.
- Omikroon will not be able to pass on the higher metal expense to its customers.

Exhibit 1: Omikroon's Selected Financial Forecasts for 2020 Base Case (€ millions)

	Petrol Scooter Division	Commercial Truck Division	Electric Scooter Division	Total
Sales	99.05	45.71	7.62	152.38
Cost of sales				105.38
Gross profit				47.00
Operating profit				9.20

Omikroon will initially outsource its electric scooter parts. But manufacturing these parts in-house beginning in 2021 will imply changes to an existing factory. This factory cost EUR7 million three years ago and had an estimated useful life of 10 years. Fromm is evaluating two scenarios:

- Sell the existing factory for EUR5 million. Build a new factory costing EUR30 million with a useful life of 10 years.
- Refit the existing factory for EUR27 million.

15. Using Porter's five forces analysis, which of the following competitive factors is likely to have the *greatest* impact on Omikroon's petrol scooter pricing power?
    A. Rivalry
    B. Threat of substitutes
    C. Threat of new entrants

16. The metric used by Fromm to assess Omikroon's performance takes into account:
    A. degree of financial leverage.
    B. operating liabilities relative to operating assets.
    C. competitiveness relative to companies in other tax regimes.

17. Based on Omikroon's expectations, the gross profit margin of Omikroon's electric scooter division in 2021 is *most likely* to be affected by:
    A. competition.
    B. research costs.
    C. cannibalization by petrol scooters.

18. Which factor *best* justifies the five-year forecast horizon for Omikroon selected by Fromm?
    A. Factor 1
    B. Factor 2
    C. Factor 3

19. Fromm's sensitivity analysis will result in a decrease in the 2020 base case gross profit margin *closest to*:
    A. 0.55 percentage points.
    B. 0.80 percentage points.
    C. 3.32 percentage points.

20. Fromm's estimate of growth capital expenditure included in Omikroon's PP&E under Scenario 2 should be:
    A. lower than under Scenario 1.
    B. the same as under Scenario 1.
    C. higher than under Scenario 1.

21. To validate the forecast for rapid growth in the electronic scooter market over the next 10 years, Fromm speaks to the management of Omikroon and investor relations of ZeroWheel, a competitor. Fromm might be subject to which behavioral bias?
    A. Conservatism
    B. Overconfidence
    C. Confirmation

CHAPTER 14

CORPORATE RESTRUCTURINGS

LEARNING OUTCOMES

The candidate should be able to:

- explain types of corporate restructurings and issuers' motivations for pursuing them
- explain the initial evaluation of a corporate restructuring
- demonstrate valuation methods for, and interpret valuations of, companies involved in corporate restructurings
- demonstrate how corporate restructurings affect an issuer's EPS, net debt to EBITDA ratio, and weighted average cost of capital
- evaluate corporate investment actions, including equity investments, joint ventures, and acquisitions
- evaluate corporate divestment actions, including sales and spin offs
- evaluate cost and balance sheet restructurings

SUMMARY

- Corporate issuers seek to alter their destiny, as described by the corporate life cycle, by taking actions known as restructurings.
- Restructurings include investment actions that increase the size and scope of an issuer's business, divestment actions that decrease size or scope, and restructuring actions that do not affect scope but improve performance.
- Investment actions include equity investments, joint ventures, and acquisitions. Investment actions are often made by issuers seeking growth, synergies, or undervalued targets.
- Divestment actions include sales and spin offs and are made by issuers seeking to increase growth or profitability or reduce risk by shedding certain divisions and assets.
- Restructuring actions, including cost cutting, balance sheet restructurings, and reorganizations, do not change the size or scope of issuers but are aimed at improving returns on capital to historical or peer levels.
- The evaluation of a corporate restructuring is composed of four phases: initial evaluation, preliminary evaluation, modeling, and updating the investment thesis. The entire evaluation is generally done only for material restructurings.

- The initial evaluation of a corporate restructuring answers the following questions: What is happening? When is it happening? Is it material? And why is it happening?
- Materiality is defined by both size and fit. One rule of thumb for size is that large actions are those that are greater than 10% of an issuer's enterprise value (e.g., for an acquisition, consideration in excess of 10% of the acquirer's pre-announcement enterprise value). Fit refers to the alignment between the action and an analyst's expectations for the issuer.
- Three common valuation methods for companies involved in corporate restructurings, during the preliminary valuation phase of the evaluation, are comparable company, comparable transaction, and premium paid analysis.
- Corporate restructurings must be modeled on the financial statements based on the situational specifics. Estimated financial statements that include the effect of a restructuring are known as pro forma financial statements.
- The weighted average cost of capital for an issuer is determined by the weights of different capital types and the constituent costs of capital. The costs of capital are influenced by both bottom-up and top-down drivers. Bottom-up drivers include stability, profitability, leverage, and asset specificity. Corporate restructurings affect the cost of capital by affecting these drivers.

PRACTICE PROBLEMS

The following information relates to questions 1–5

Jane Chang is an analyst at Alpha Fund covering the real estate and energy sectors. She and her colleague are analyzing two companies that are currently held by the fund.

The first company is Jupiter Corp., a publicly traded, national retail grocery store chain that has 2,800 physical stores. Jupiter leases most of its grocery stores and all five of its office locations that help the company achieve its core business of operating 50,000 square foot stores in all markets of the United States. Jupiter also owns the real estate (land and building) associated with 100 physical store locations. Jupiter recently announced that its board of directors approved a strategic real estate plan to pursue a separation of all its owned assets. The company currently has a speculative-grade credit rating.

The separation would be achieved through a series of sale-leaseback transactions with real estate investment trusts (REITs) that specialize in owning retail properties. Under the plan, Jupiter will sell its 100 owned grocery stores and lease them for 15-year terms with a combined annual rent expense of USD40 million. Jupiter expects to receive cash proceeds of approximately USD800 million from the property sales, which will be used to retire approximately USD600 million of debt and repurchase 4 million common shares.

Jupiter believes the pro forma capital structure following the transactions will enable it to receive an investment-grade credit rating. The sale-leaseback transactions value the 100 assets at an average capitalization rate of 5.50%. Based on Chang's colleague's research, the 25th, 50th, and 75th percentile cap rates for sale transactions for similarly situated properties and similar lease terms in the last three years were 5.00%, 5.50%, and 6.00%, respectively.

The second company is Saturn Corp., a publicly traded US energy company. Chang has been asked to assess the valuation of a potential spin off for this company. Saturn operates and reports three segments: Upstream, Midstream, and Downstream. In the last 12 months, the company reported the financial results shown in Exhibit 1.

EXHIBIT 1

Segment	EBITDA (USD Millions)
Upstream	14,400
Midstream	5,760
Downstream	3,840
Consolidated	**24,000**

Saturn is currently trading at an enterprise value of USD408,000 million, or an EV/EBITDA multiple of 17. A spin off of the Downstream segment has long been rumored because it has been under-invested in by the current management team, resulting in slower revenue growth than its peers. Chang finds that the median Upstream, Midstream, and Downstream peers are trading at enterprise value-to-EBITDA multiples of 19, 17, and 13, respectively.

During an internal discussion, Chang's colleague makes the following three statements about the comparable company analysis method:

Statement 1: The method is not sensitive to market mispricing.

Statement 2: The estimates of value are derived directly from the market.

Statement 3: The method provides a reasonable approximation of a target company's value relative to similar transactions in the market.

1. Jupiter's strategic real estate plan would be best characterized as a:
   A. reorganization.
   B. cost restructuring.
   C. balance sheet restructuring.

2. Which of the following statements about Jupiter's motivations for the strategic real estate plan is incorrect?
   A. The transactions will enable Jupiter to sell a non-core business.
   B. The transactions will allow Jupiter to unlock the value of its real estate assets.
   C. The expected change in Jupiter's credit rating after the transactions will increase the firm's costs of capital.

3. Which of the following statements *best* describes Jupiter's average capitalization rate for the sale-leaseback transactions? Jupiter's average capitalization rate:
   A. is supported by the comparable transactions.
   B. compares favorably to the comparable transactions.
   C. compares unfavorably to the comparable transactions.

4. Based on Exhibit 1 and the peer median EV/EBITDA multiples, Saturn's estimated enterprise value is *closest* to:
   A. USD392,000 million.
   B. USD408,000 million.
   C. USD421,440 million.

5. Which of Chang's colleague's three statements is correct?
   A. Statement 1
   B. Statement 2
   C. Statement 3

The following information relates to questions 6–10

Elaine Lee is an analyst at an investment bank covering the energy sector. She and her junior analyst are analyzing Stratton Oil Corporation.

Stratton Oil Corporation is a publicly traded, US-based energy company that just announced its acquisition of Midwest Oil Corporation, a smaller US-based energy company. Stratton will pay USD55 in cash and 2.25 Stratton shares for each Midwest share, for a total consideration of USD40 billion based on share prices just prior to the announcement. Stratton's current trading enterprise value just prior to the announcement was USD170 billion. Lee concludes that the acquisition does not signal a change in strategy or focus for Stratton.

Stratton expects to realize annual recurring cost synergies of USD350 million (pre-tax), primarily from efficiencies in oil exploration and production activities and savings in corporate costs. The achievement of the full USD350 million in synergies is expected by the end of the third year after the acquisition closes. Synergies are realized in the amounts of USD117 million, USD233 million, and USD350 million in Years 1–3, respectively, and cash costs of USD175 million, USD280 million, and USD395 million are incurred in Years 1–3, respectively.

Expectations for revenues and total operating expenses for Stratton and Midwest for the next three years prior to the acquisition announcement are shown in Exhibit 1.

EXHIBIT 1: Stratton and Midwest Year 1–3 Figures, Prior to Acquisition (USD millions)

Stratton	Year 1	Year 2	Year 3
Revenues	21,325	22,391	23,511
Operating expenses	16,525	17,351	18,219
Midwest			
Revenues	5,350	5,618	5,898
Operating expenses	3,050	3,203	3,363

Lee's junior analyst makes the following comment during a conversation with Lee:

The acquisition is considered immaterial in the initial evaluation step for Stratton because it does not signal a change in strategy or focus.

Stratton's offer valued Midwest at an enterprise value of USD40.6 billion, including USD4.3 billion of existing Midwest debt. To finance the consideration of USD55 in cash and 2.25 Stratton shares for each Midwest share, Stratton will issue 104 million new shares and raise approximately USD26 billion in new debt and fund the remainder with cash on hand. Following the close, Stratton expects its outstanding debt will be approximately USD62 billion. Prior to the acquisition, Stratton has 1.096 billion shares outstanding trading at USD125 per share. Lee wants to determine how much the weights of debt and equity in

Stratton's capital structure will change assuming a constant share price and that the book value of debt equals its market value.

During an internal meeting, Lee asks if Stratton could have achieved its same goals by undertaking an equity investment or joint venture. In response, Lee's junior analyst makes the following three statements.

Statement 1: Acquisitions require substantially greater capital investments than equity investments.

Statement 2: Acquisitions and equity investments are similar in that they both allow the acquirer to gain control of the target.

Statement 3: Relative to joint ventures, equity investments provide more equal governance representation and require larger investments.

Lee conducted a sum-of-the-parts valuation of Stratton's three segments and calculated an estimated enterprise value of USD187 billion just prior to the announcement.

6. Based on Exhibit 1, the forecasted operating income in Year 3 for the combined Stratton and Midwest is *closest* to:
   A. USD7,432.
   B. USD7,782.
   C. USD8,177.

7. Lee's junior analyst's comment about materiality is:
   A. correct.
   B. incorrect because the acquisition is considered a small acquisition.
   C. incorrect because the acquisition represents more than 10% of Stratton's enterprise value prior to the transaction.

8. The weight of equity in Stratton's capital structure as a result of the acquisition of Midwest assuming Lee's two assumptions is closest to:
   A. 29%.
   B. 71%.
   C. 81%.

9. Which of Lee's junior analyst's three statements is correct?
   A. Statement 1
   B. Statement 2
   C. Statement 3

10. Stratton's estimated conglomerate discount just prior to the announcement is:
    A. −USD17 billion.
    B. USD0.
    C. USD17 billion.

ENVIRONMENTAL, SOCIAL, AND GOVERNANCE (ESG) CONSIDERATIONS IN INVESTMENT ANALYSIS

LEARNING OUTCOMES

The candidate should be able to:

- describe global variations in ownership structures and the possible effects of these variations on corporate governance policies and practices
- evaluate the effectiveness of a company's corporate governance policies and practices
- describe how ESG-related risk exposures and investment opportunities may be identified and evaluated
- evaluate ESG risk exposures and investment opportunities related to a company

SUMMARY

- Shareholder ownership structures are commonly classified as dispersed, concentrated, or a hybrid of the two.
- Dispersed ownership reflects the existence of many shareholders, none of which, either individually or collectively, has the ability to exercise control over the corporation. Concentrated corporate ownership reflects an individual shareholder or a group (controlling shareholders) with the ability to exercise control over the corporation.
- Controlling shareholders may be either majority shareholders or minority shareholders.
- Horizontal ownership involves companies with mutual business interests that have cross-holding share arrangements with each other. Vertical (or pyramid) ownership involves a company or group that has a controlling interest in two or more holding companies, which in turn have controlling interests in various operating companies.
- Dual-class (or multiple-class) shares grant one or more share classes superior or even sole voting rights while other share classes have inferior or no voting rights.

- Types of influential owners include banks, families, sovereign governments, institutional investors, group companies, private equity firms, foreign investors, managers, and board directors.
- A corporation's board of directors is typically structured as either one tier or two tier. A one-tier board consists of a single board of directors, composed of executive (internal) and non-executive (external) directors. A two-tier board consists of a supervisory board that oversees a management board.
- CEO duality exists when the chief executive officer also serves as chairperson of the board.
- A primary challenge of integrating ESG factors into investment analysis is identifying and obtaining information that is relevant, comparable, and decision-useful.
- ESG information and metrics are inconsistently reported by companies, and such disclosure is voluntary, which provides additional challenges for analysts.
- In an ESG context, materiality typically refers to ESG-related issues that are expected to affect a company's operations or financial performance and the valuation of its securities.
- Corporate governance considerations, such as the structure of the board of directors, tend to be reasonably consistent across most companies. In contrast, environmental and social considerations often differ greatly.
- Analysts typically use three main sources of information to identify a company's (or industry's) ESG factors: (1) proprietary research, (2) ratings and analysis from ESG data providers, or (3) research from not-for-profit industry organizations and initiatives.
- In equity analysis, ESG integration is used to both identify potential opportunities and mitigate downside risk, whereas in fixed-income analysis, ESG integration is generally focused on mitigating downside risk.
- A typical starting point for ESG integration is the identification of material qualitative and quantitative ESG factors that pertain to a company or its industry.

PRACTICE PROBLEMS

The following information relates to questions 1–6

Theresa Blass manages the Toptier Balanced Fund (the Fund) and recently hired John Yorkton, a junior analyst, to help her research investment opportunities. Blass plans to integrate environmental, social, and governance (ESG) factors into her analysis. She is researching an equity investment in Titian International, a global steel producer. She asks Yorkton to identify ESG factors impacting Titian and estimate the equity valuation for the company. Yorkton uses proprietary methods to identify the ESG factors.

Yorkton points out that Titian's steel production is energy intensive and relies on coal in producing its main product, stainless steel. The firm's major customers are oil and gas firms using stainless steel in their drilling operations. Most of Titian's steel capacity is located in developing economies, where it currently faces few environmental regulations. Titian has a 10-member board with a chairperson and 5 independent members. The chairperson is not the CEO, and the board is diverse, with 6 women. The company has an excellent record on employee health and safety. In a discussion with Blass about ESG factors in investment analysis, Yorkton makes the following statements:

Statement 1 Material ESG information used in investment analysis is best obtained from the individual companies.

Statement 2 The level of disclosure varies among companies because these disclosures are voluntary.

Statement 3 The time horizon has little effect on the materiality of the underlying ESG factors.

Yorkton integrates ESG factors into the equity valuation of Titian. He believes the company faces significant long-term risk due to regulatory changes regarding greenhouse gas emissions in the developing economies. These changes will have a negative impact on Titian's steel capacity and its production costs. Based on long-term forecasts from the International Energy Agency (IEA), Yorkton expects oil and natural gas demand to decline over the next decade, reducing oil company capital expenditures on exploration and drilling. He uses a discounted cash flow model to value Titian stock.

1. The potential problem with Yorkton's approach to identifying ESG factors is the:
   A. promotion of uniform accounting standards.
   B. subjective assessment of ESG scores and rankings.
   C. inconsistent reporting of ESG information and metrics among firms.

2. The most relevant industry risk factors affecting Titian are:
   A. social.
   B. governance.
   C. environmental.

3. Which of the statements made by Yorkton on ESG factors in investment analysis is correct?
   A. Statement 1
   B. Statement 2
   C. Statement 3

4. Titian faces long-term risk from _____ due to potential regulatory changes in the developing economies.

5. Yorkton's ESG integration approach is likely to impact equity valuation by:
   A. increasing revenues.
   B. raising the discount rate.
   C. reducing operating costs.

6. After integrating the ESG factors into the discounted cash flow model, the equity value of Titian is likely to:
   A. decrease.
   B. remain unchanged.
   C. increase.

The following information relates to questions 7–10

Emily Marker, CFA, is a fixed-income analyst for the Namsan Funds. Her supervisor asks her to identify ESG factors and value the corporate bonds of BR Hotels, a publicly traded boutique hotel company. Marker notes that BR Hotels is a "green hotel" company that prioritizes sustainability and has successfully reduced water and energy usage at its hotels. The founding family owns 55% of the outstanding shares. Each ownership share has equivalent voting rights. The board of directors of BR Hotels consists of 15 members, with independent CEO and chairperson roles. The board includes one independent member and two women, and 20% of the board members have experience in the hotel industry.

BR Hotels has historically had a high labor turnover rate. Most of its workforce are paid at or near the minimum wage, and the company offers no health benefits. Marker and her supervisor discuss how BR Hotels will be affected by the expected passage of legislation raising the minimum wage and growing pressure to offer benefits. Marker integrates ESG factors in the investment valuation of BR Hotels' corporate bonds.

7. The potential conflict between or among shareholders and managers of BR Hotels can *best* be described as:
    A. voting caps.
    B. a principal-agent problem.
    C. a principal-principal problem.

8. BR Hotels' corporate governance risk is increased by:
    A. CEO duality.
    B. family control.
    C. the low percentage of independent board members.

9. The security analysis of BR Hotels is *most likely* focused on:
    A. mitigating downside risk.
    B. adjusting the discount rate.
    C. identifying potential opportunities.

10. After integrating the ESG factors, the credit spread on BR Hotels' bonds is *most likely* to:
    A. decrease.
    B. remain unchanged.
    C. increase.

CHAPTER 16

INTERCORPORATE INVESTMENTS

LEARNING OUTCOMES

The candidate should be able to:

- describe the classification, measurement, and disclosure under International Financial Reporting Standards (IFRS) for 1) investments in financial assets, 2) investments in associates, 3) joint ventures, 4) business combinations, and 5) special purpose and variable interest entities
- compare and contrast IFRS and US GAAP in their classification, measurement, and disclosure of investments in financial assets, investments in associates, joint ventures, business combinations, and special purpose and variable interest entities
- analyze how different methods used to account for intercorporate investments affect financial statements and ratios

SUMMARY

Intercompany investments play a significant role in business activities and create significant challenges for the analyst in assessing company performance. Investments in other companies can take five basic forms: investments in financial assets, investments in associates, joint ventures, business combinations, and investments in special purpose and variable interest entities. Key concepts are as follows:

- Investments in financial assets are those in which the investor has no significant influence. They can be measured and reported as

  - Fair value through profit or loss.
  - Fair value through other comprehensive income.
  - Amortized cost.

  IFRS and US GAAP treat investments in financial assets in a similar manner.
- Investments in associates and joint ventures are those in which the investor has significant influence, but not control, over the investee's business activities. Because the investor can

exert significant influence over financial and operating policy decisions, IFRS and US GAAP require the equity method of accounting because it provides a more objective basis for reporting investment income.

- The equity method requires the investor to recognize income as earned rather than when dividends are received.
- The equity investment is carried at cost, plus its share of post-acquisition income (after adjustments) less dividends received.
- The equity investment is reported as a single line item on the balance sheet and on the income statement.

- IFRS and US GAAP accounting standards require the use of the acquisition method to account for business combinations. Fair value of the consideration given is the appropriate measurement for identifiable assets and liabilities acquired in the business combination.
- Goodwill is the difference between the acquisition value and the fair value of the target's identifiable net tangible and intangible assets. Because it is considered to have an indefinite life, it is not amortized. Instead, it is evaluated at least annually for impairment. Impairment losses are reported on the income statement. IFRS use a one-step approach to determine and measure the impairment loss, whereas US GAAP uses a two-step approach.
- If the acquiring company acquires less than 100%, non-controlling (minority) shareholders' interests are reported on the consolidated financial statements. IFRS allows the non-controlling interest to be measured at either its fair value (full goodwill) or at the non-controlling interest's proportionate share of the acquiree's identifiable net assets (partial goodwill). US GAAP requires the non-controlling interest to be measured at fair value (full goodwill).
- Consolidated financial statements are prepared in each reporting period.
- Special purpose entities (SPEs) and variable interest entities (VIEs) are required to be consolidated by the entity, which is expected to absorb the majority of the expected losses or receive the majority of expected residual benefits.

PRACTICE PROBLEMS

The following information relates to questions 1–6

Burton Howard, CFA, is an equity analyst with Maplewood Securities. Howard is preparing a research report on Confabulated Materials, SA, a publicly traded company based in France that complies with IFRS 9. As part of his analysis, Howard has assembled data gathered from the financial statement footnotes of Confabulated's 2018 Annual Report and from discussions with company management. Howard is concerned about the effect of this information on Confabulated's future earnings.

Information about Confabulated's investment portfolio for the years ended 31 December 2017 and 2018 is presented in Exhibit 1. As part of his research, Howard is considering the possible effect on reported income of Confabulated's accounting classification for fixed income investments.

EXHIBIT 1: Confabulated's Investment Portfolio (€ Thousands)

Characteristic	Bugle AG	Cathay Corp	Dumas SA
Classification	FVPL	FVOCI	Amortized cost
Cost*	€25,000	€40,000	€50,000
Market value, 31 December 2017	29,000	38,000	54,000
Market value, 31 December 2018	28,000	37,000	55,000

* All securities were acquired at par value.

In addition, Confabulated's annual report discusses a transaction under which receivables were securitized through a special purpose entity (SPE) for Confabulated's benefit.

1. The balance sheet carrying value of Confabulated's investment portfolio (in € thousands) at 31 December 2018 is *closest* to:
    A. 112,000.
    B. 115,000.
    C. 118,000.

2. The balance sheet carrying value of Confabulated's investment portfolio at 31 December 2018 would have been higher if which of the securities had been reclassified as FVPL security?
    A. Bugle.
    B. Cathay.
    C. Dumas.

3. Compared to Confabulated's reported interest income in 2018, if Dumas had been classified as FVPL, the interest income would have been:
    A. lower.
    B. the same.
    C. higher.

4. Compared to Confabulated's reported earnings before taxes in 2018, if Dumas had been classified as a FVPL security, the earnings before taxes (in € thousands) would have been:
    A. the same.
    B. €1,000 lower.
    C. €1,000 higher.

5. Confabulated's reported interest income would be lower if the cost was the same but the par value (in € thousands) of:
    A. Bugle was €28,000.
    B. Cathay was €37,000.
    C. Dumas was €55,000.

6. Confabulated's special purpose entity is *most likely* to be:
    A. held off-balance-sheet.
    B. consolidated on Confabulated's financial statements.
    C. consolidated on Confabulated's financial statements only if it is a "qualifying SPE."

The following information relates to questions 7–11

Cinnamon, Inc. is a diversified manufacturing company headquartered in the United Kingdom. It complies with IFRS. In 2017, Cinnamon held a 19 percent passive equity ownership interest in Cambridge Processing. In December 2017, Cinnamon announced that it would be increasing its ownership interest to 50 percent effective 1 January 2018 through a cash purchase. Cinnamon and Cambridge have no intercompany transactions.

Peter Lubbock, an analyst following both Cinnamon and Cambridge, is curious how the increased stake will affect Cinnamon's consolidated financial statements. He asks Cinnamon's CFO how the company will account for the investment, and is told that the decision has not yet been made. Lubbock decides to use his existing forecasts for both companies' financial statements to compare the outcomes of alternative accounting treatments.

Lubbock assembles abbreviated financial statement data for Cinnamon (Exhibit 1) and Cambridge (Exhibit 2) for this purpose.

EXHIBIT 1: Selected Financial Statement Information for Cinnamon, Inc. (£ Millions)

Year Ending 31 December	2017	2018*
Revenue	1,400	1,575
Operating income	126	142
Net income	62	69
31 December	**2017**	**2018***
Total assets	1,170	1,317
Shareholders' equity	616	685

* Estimates made prior to announcement of increased stake in Cambridge.

EXHIBIT 2: Selected Financial Statement Information for Cambridge Processing (£ Millions)

Year Ending 31 December	2017	2018*
Revenue	1,000	1,100
Operating income	80	88
Net income	40	44
Dividends paid	20	22
31 December	**2017**	**2018***
Total assets	800	836
Shareholders' equity	440	462

* Estimates made prior to announcement of increased stake by Cinnamon.

7. In 2018, if Cinnamon is deemed to have control over Cambridge, it will *most likely* account for its investment in Cambridge using:
   A. the equity method.
   B. the acquisition method.
   C. proportionate consolidation.

8. At 31 December 2018, Cinnamon's total shareholders' equity on its balance sheet would *most likely* be:
   A. highest if Cinnamon is deemed to have control of Cambridge.
   B. independent of the accounting method used for the investment in Cambridge.
   C. highest if Cinnamon is deemed to have significant influence over Cambridge.

9. In 2018, Cinnamon's net profit margin would be *highest* if:
   A. it is deemed to have control of Cambridge.
   B. it had not increased its stake in Cambridge.
   C. it is deemed to have significant influence over Cambridge.

10. At 31 December 2018, assuming control and recognition of goodwill, Cinnamon's reported debt to equity ratio will *most likely* be highest if it accounts for its investment in Cambridge using the:
    A. equity method.
    B. full goodwill method.
    C. partial goodwill method.

11. Compared to Cinnamon's operating margin in 2017, if it is deemed to have control of Cambridge, its operating margin in 2018 will *most likely* be:
    A. lower.
    B. higher.
    C. the same.

The following information relates to questions 12–16

Zimt, AG is a consumer products manufacturer headquartered in Austria. It complies with IFRS. In 2017, Zimt held a 10 percent passive stake in Oxbow Limited. In December 2017, Zimt announced that it would be increasing its ownership to 50 percent effective 1 January 2018.

Franz Gelblum, an analyst following both Zimt and Oxbow, is curious how the increased stake will affect Zimt's consolidated financial statements. Because Gelblum is uncertain how the company will account for the increased stake, he uses his existing forecasts for both companies' financial statements to compare various alternative outcomes.

Gelblum gathers abbreviated financial statement data for Zimt (Exhibit 1) and Oxbow (Exhibit 2) for this purpose.

EXHIBIT 1: Selected Financial Statement Estimates for Zimt AG (€ Millions)

Year Ending 31 December	2017	2018*
Revenue	1,500	1,700
Operating income	135	153
Net income	66	75
31 December	2017	2018*
Total assets	1,254	1,421
Shareholders' equity	660	735

* Estimates made prior to announcement of increased stake in Oxbow.

EXHIBIT 2: Selected Financial Statement Estimates for Oxbow Limited (€ Millions)

Year Ending 31 December	2017	2018*
Revenue	1,200	1,350
Operating income	120	135
Net income	60	68
Dividends paid	20	22

31 December	2017	2018*
Total assets	1,200	1,283
Shareholders' equity	660	706

* Estimates made prior to announcement of increased stake by Zimt.

12. At 31 December 2018, Zimt's total assets balance would *most likely* be:
    A. highest if Zimt is deemed to have control of Oxbow.
    B. highest if Zimt is deemed to have significant influence over Oxbow.
    C. unaffected by the accounting method used for the investment in Oxbow.

13. Based on Gelblum's estimates, if Zimt is deemed to have significant influence over Oxbow, its 2018 net income (in € millions) would be *closest* to:
    A. €75.
    B. €109.
    C. €143.

14. Based on Gelblum's estimates, if Zimt is deemed to have joint control of Oxbow, and Zimt uses the proportionate consolidation method, its 31 December 2018 total liabilities (in € millions) will *most likely* be *closest* to:
    A. €686.
    B. €975.
    C. €1,263.

15. Based on Gelblum's estimates, if Zimt is deemed to have control over Oxbow, its 2018 consolidated sales (in € millions) will be *closest* to:
    A. €1,700.
    B. €2,375.
    C. €3,050.

16. Based on Gelblum's estimates, and holding the size of Zimt's ownership stake in Oxbow constant, Zimt's net income in 2018 will *most likely* be:
    A. highest if Zimt is deemed to have control of Oxbow.
    B. highest if Zimt is deemed to have significant influence over Oxbow.
    C. independent of the accounting method used for the investment in Oxbow.

The following information relates to questions 17–22

BetterCare Hospitals, Inc. operates a chain of hospitals throughout the United States. The company has been expanding by acquiring local hospitals. Its largest acquisition, that of Statewide Medical, was made in 2001 under the pooling of interests method. BetterCare complies with US GAAP.

BetterCare is currently forming a 50/50 joint venture with Supreme Healthcare under which the companies will share control of several hospitals. BetterCare plans to use the equity method to account for the joint venture. Supreme Healthcare complies with IFRS and will use the proportionate consolidation method to account for the joint venture.

Erik Ohalin is an equity analyst who covers both companies. He has estimated the joint venture's financial information for 2018 in order to prepare his estimates of each company's earnings and financial performance. This information is presented in Exhibit 1.

EXHIBIT 1: Selected Financial Statement Forecasts for Joint Venture ($ Millions)

Year Ending 31 December	2018
Revenue	1,430
Operating income	128
Net income	62
31 December	**2018**
Total assets	1,500
Shareholders' equity	740

Supreme Healthcare recently announced it had formed a special purpose entity through which it plans to sell up to $100 million of its accounts receivable. Supreme Healthcare has no voting interest in the SPE, but it is expected to absorb any losses that it may incur. Ohalin wants to estimate the impact this will have on Supreme Healthcare's consolidated financial statements.

17. Compared to accounting principles currently in use, the pooling method BetterCare used for its Statewide Medical acquisition has *most likely* caused its reported:
    A. revenue to be higher.
    B. total equity to be lower.
    C. total assets to be higher.

18. Based on Ohalin's estimates, the amount of joint venture revenue (in $ millions) included on BetterCare's consolidated 2018 financial statements should be *closest* to:
    A. $0.
    B. $715.
    C. $1,430.

19. Based on Ohalin's estimates, the amount of joint venture net income included on the consolidated financial statements of each venturer will *most likely* be:
    A. higher for BetterCare.
    B. higher for Supreme Healthcare.
    C. the same for both BetterCare and Supreme Healthcare.

20. Based on Ohalin's estimates, the amount of the joint venture's 31 December 2018 total assets (in $ millions) that will be included on Supreme Healthcare's consolidated financial statements will be *closest* to:
    A. $0.
    B. $750.
    C. $1,500.

21. Based on Ohalin's estimates, the amount of joint venture shareholders' equity at 31 December 2018 included on the consolidated financial statements of each venturer will *most likely* be:
    A. higher for BetterCare.
    B. higher for Supreme Healthcare.
    C. the same for both BetterCare and Supreme Healthcare.

22. If Supreme Healthcare sells its receivables to the SPE, its consolidated financial results will *least likely* show:
    A. a higher revenue for 2018.
    B. the same cash balance at 31 December 2018.
    C. the same accounts receivable balance at 31 December 2018.

The following information relates to questions 23–29

John Thronen is an analyst in the research department of an international securities firm. Thronen is preparing a research report on Topmaker, Inc., a publicly-traded company that complies with IFRS. Thronen reviews two of Topmaker's recent transactions relating to investments in Blanco Co. and Rainer Co.

Investment in Blanca Co.

On 1 January 2016, Topmaker invested $11 million in Blanca Co. debt securities (with a 5.0% stated coupon rate on par value, payable each 31 December). The par value of the securities is $10 million, and the market interest rate in effect when the bonds were purchased was 4.0%. Topmaker designates the investment as held-to-maturity. On 31 December 2016, the fair value of the securities was $12 million.

Blanca Co. plans to raise $40 million in capital by borrowing against its financial receivables. Blanca plans to create a special purpose entity (SPE), invest $10 million in the SPE, have the SPE borrow $40 million, and then use the total funds to purchase $50 million of receivables from Blanca. Blanca meets the definition of control and plans to consolidate the SPE. Blanca's current balance sheet is presented in Exhibit 1.

EXHIBIT 1: Blanca Co. Balance Sheet at 31 December 2016 ($ millions)

Cash	20	Current liabilities	25
Accounts receivable	50	Noncurrent liabilities	30
Other assets	30	Shareholders' equity	45
Total assets	**100**	**Total liabilities and equity**	**100**

Investment in Rainer Co.

On 1 January 2016, Topmaker acquired a 15% equity interest with voting power in Rainer Co. for $300 million. Exhibit 2 presents selected financial information for Rainer on the acquisition date. Thronen notes that the plant and equipment are depreciated on a straight-line basis and have 10 years of remaining life. Topmaker has representation on Rainer's board of directors and participates in the associate's policy-making process.

EXHIBIT 2: Selected Financial Data for Rainer Co., 1 January 2018 (Acquisition Date) ($ millions)

	Book Value	Fair Value
Current assets	270	270
Plant and equipment	2,900	3,160
Total assets	3,170	3,430
Liabilities	1,830	1,830
Net assets	1,340	1,600

Thronen notes that, for fiscal year 2018, Rainer reported total revenue of $1,740 million and net income of $360 million, and paid dividends of $220 million.

Thronen is concerned about possible goodwill impairment for Topmaker due to expected changes in the industry effective at the end of 2017. He calculates the impairment loss based on selected data from the projected consolidated balance sheet data presented in Exhibit 3, assuming that the cash-generating unit and reporting unit of Topmaker are the same.

EXHIBIT 3: Selected Financial Data for Topmaker, Inc., Estimated Year Ending 31 December 2017 ($ millions)

Carrying value of cash-generating unit/reporting unit	15,200
Recoverable amount of cash-generating unit/reporting unit	14,900
Fair value of reporting unit	14,800
Identifiable net assets	14,400
Goodwill	520

Finally, Topmaker announces its plan to increase its ownership interest in Rainer to 80% effective 1 January 2018 and will account for the investment in Rainer using the partial goodwill method. Thronen estimates that the fair market value of the Rainer's shares on the expected date of exchange is $2 billion with the identifiable assets valued at $1.5 billion.

23. The carrying value of Topmaker's investment in Blanca's debt securities reported on the balance sheet at 31 December 2016 is:
    A. $10.94 million.
    B. $11.00 million.
    C. $12.00 million.

24. Based on Exhibit 1 and Blanca's plans to borrow against its financial receivables, the new consolidated balance sheet will show total assets of:
    A. $50 million.
    B. $140 million.
    C. $150 million.

25. Based on Exhibit 2, Topmaker's investment in Rainer resulted in goodwill of:
    A. $21 million.
    B. $60 million.
    C. $99 million.

26. Topmaker's influence on Rainer's business activities can be *best* described as:
    A. significant.
    B. controlling.
    C. shared control.

27. Using only the information from Exhibit 2, the carrying value of Topmaker's investment in Rainer at the end of 2016 is *closest* to:
    A. $282 million.
    B. $317 million.
    C. $321 million.

28. Based on Exhibit 3, Topmaker's impairment loss under IFRS is:
    A. $120 million.
    B. $300 million.
    C. $400 million.

29. Based on Thronen's value estimates on the acquisition date of 1 January 2018, the estimated value of the minority interest related to Rainer will be:
    A. $300 million.
    B. $400 million.
    C. $500 million.

The following information relates to questions 30–35

Percy Byron, CFA, is an equity analyst with a UK-based investment firm. One firm Byron follows is NinMount PLC, a UK-based company. On 31 December 2018, NinMount paid £320 million to purchase a 50 percent stake in Boswell Company. The excess of the purchase price over the fair value of Boswell's net assets was attributable to previously unrecorded licenses. These licenses were estimated to have an economic life of six years. The fair value of Boswell's assets and liabilities other than licenses was equal to their recorded book values. NinMount and Boswell both use the pound sterling as their reporting currency and prepare their financial statements in accordance with IFRS.

Byron is concerned whether the investment should affect his "buy" rating on NinMount common stock. He knows NinMount could choose one of several accounting methods to report the results of its investment, but NinMount has not announced which method it will use. Byron forecasts that both companies' 2019 financial results (excluding any merger accounting adjustments) will be identical to those of 2018.

NinMount's and Boswell's condensed income statements for the year ended 31 December 2018, and condensed balance sheets at 31 December 2018, are presented in Exhibits 1 and 2, respectively.

EXHIBIT 1: NinMount PLC and Boswell Company Income Statements for the Year Ended 31 December 2018 (£ millions)

	NinMount	Boswell
Net sales	950	510
Cost of goods sold	(495)	(305)
Selling expenses	(50)	(15)
Administrative expenses	(136)	(49)
Depreciation & amortization expense	(102)	(92)
Interest expense	(42)	(32)
Income before taxes	125	17
Income tax expense	(50)	(7)
Net income	75	10

EXHIBIT 2: NinMount PLC and Boswell Company Balance Sheets at 31 December 2018 (£ millions)

	NinMount	Boswell
Cash	50	20
Receivables—net	70	45
Inventory	130	75
Total current assets	250	140
Property, plant, & equipment—net	1,570	930
Investment in Boswell	320	—
Total assets	2,140	1,070
Current liabilities	110	90
Long-term debt	600	400
Total liabilities	710	490
Common stock	850	535
Retained earnings	580	45
Total equity	1,430	580
Total liabilities and equity	2,140	1,070

Note: Balance sheets reflect the purchase price paid by NinMount, but do not yet consider the impact of the accounting method choice.

30. NinMount's current ratio on 31 December 2018 *most likely* will be highest if the results of the acquisition are reported using:
    A. the equity method.
    B. consolidation with full goodwill.
    C. consolidation with partial goodwill.

31. NinMount's long-term debt to equity ratio on 31 December 2018 *most likely* will be lowest if the results of the acquisition are reported using:
    A. the equity method.
    B. consolidation with full goodwill.
    C. consolidation with partial goodwill.

32. Based on Byron's forecast, if NinMount deems it has acquired control of Boswell, NinMount's consolidated 2019 depreciation and amortization expense (in £ millions) will be *closest* to:
    A. 102.
    B. 148.
    C. 204.

33. Based on Byron's forecast, NinMount's net profit margin for 2019 *most likely* will be highest if the results of the acquisition are reported using:
    A. the equity method.
    B. consolidation with full goodwill.
    C. consolidation with partial goodwill.

34. Based on Byron's forecast, NinMount's 2019 return on beginning equity *most likely* will be the same under:
    A. either of the consolidations, but different under the equity method.
    B. the equity method, consolidation with full goodwill, and consolidation with partial goodwill.
    C. none of the equity method, consolidation with full goodwill, or consolidation with partial goodwill.

35. Based on Byron's forecast, NinMount's 2019 total asset turnover ratio on beginning assets under the equity method is *most likely*:
    A. lower than if the results are reported using consolidation.
    B. the same as if the results are reported using consolidation.
    C. higher than if the results are reported using consolidation.

PART II

SOLUTIONS

CHAPTER 1

CORPORATE STRUCTURES AND OWNERSHIP

SOLUTIONS

1. Private companies can go public through a process known as the initial public offering (IPO). This means that the company is offering its shares to all investors for the first time. An investment bank (or group of investment banks) acts as the underwriter of the offering, meaning that they guarantee the sale of the shares for the issuer. Once the IPO process is completed, the shares are listed on an exchange and available for trading. Another way a private company can go public is through a direct listing (DL), which is a process that does not involve underwriters or the issuance of new shares.

   Private companies can also go public indirectly by being acquired by another company that is already public or through a special purpose acquisition company (SPAC). A SPAC is a publicly-listed holding company created for the sole purpose of acquiring a private company.

2. Two common ways for public companies to go private are the leverage buyout (LBO) and management buyout (MBO). An LBO occurs when an outside investor or group of investors borrows money to purchase all of the equity of the public company. A premium to the market price must be paid to convince all shareholders to agree to the LBO. The investors typically pledge the assets of the company against the loan.

   An MBO is similar, except that the investors are part of the company's management team. Another way for a public company to go private is to be acquired by a private company. Once a company goes private, its shares are no longer listed on an exchange. A public company can also be acquired by another public company. When this happens, shares of the acquired company are delisted from the exchange; however, shares of the acquiring company remain listed.

3. B and C are correct.

   A is incorrect. If they are run well, nonprofits can generate profits; however, all profits must be reinvested in promoting the mission of the organization.

   B is correct. In contrast to public companies, private company shares do not trade on an exchange, so no visible valuation or price transparency exists for the company. Private company shares are not liquid. This means that transferring ownership from seller to buyer is more difficult than it is for a public company.

C is correct. In many countries, if there are a large number of shareholders (usually greater than 50), the company is categorized as a public company and subject to more onerous regulatory requirements whether or not it is listed on a stock exchange.

4. B is correct. From the issuer's perspective, bonds are riskier than stocks for the same reason bonds are safer than stocks for investors. Bonds increase risk to the corporation by increasing leverage. If the company is struggling and cannot meet its promised obligations to bondholders, bondholders have the legal standing to force certain actions upon the corporation, such as bankruptcy and liquidation.

5. A is correct; the statement is true. If a company fails to meet its obligation to bondholders and ultimately needs to petition the courts for bankruptcy protection, a potential alternative to asset liquidation to maximize proceeds for debt repayment is business reorganization. Following that path through the legal process as opposed to transactions in private or public markets, the company can be reorganized with shareholders getting wiped out and bondholders becoming its new shareholders.

6. From an investor's perspective, debt is less risky than equity because the company has a contractual obligation to repay the debt but no obligation to repay equity capital. Furthermore, debtholders are entitled only to the promised interest payments and the return of principal. As a result, debtholders would prefer that the company invest in relatively safe projects that produce sufficient returns to service the debt. They see no added benefit of taking greater risks that might generate larger returns. The gains to equityholders, however, are unlimited. As a result, equityholders prefer that the company invest in projects that might be riskier but that have the potential to produce much larger returns.

7. Reason 1. Mergers and acquisitions are partly responsible. When a public company is acquired by a private company or by another public company, there is one less public company.

    Reason 2. LBOs and MBOs are also responsible since they are structured to take public companies private.

    Reason 3. Many private companies choose to remain private. Greater ease in accessing capital in private markets (venture capital, private equity, and private debt) has enabled companies to source the capital they might need and avoid the regulatory burden associated with being a public company.

CHAPTER 2

INTRODUCTION TO CORPORATE GOVERNANCE AND OTHER ESG CONSIDERATIONS

SOLUTIONS

1. B is correct. Compared with other stakeholder groups, customers tend to be less affected by or concerned with a company's financial performance.

2. A is correct. Shareholder and manager interests can diverge with respect to risk tolerance. In some cases, shareholders with diversified investment portfolios can have a fairly high risk tolerance because specific company risk can be diversified away. Managers are typically more risk averse in their corporate decision making to better protect their employment status.

3. B is correct. Often, policies on related-party transactions require that such transactions or matters be voted on by the board (or shareholders), excluding the director holding the interest.

4. B is correct. The election of directors is considered an ordinary resolution and, therefore, requires only a simple majority of votes to be passed.

5. C is correct. The risks of poor corporate governance have long been understood by analysts and shareholders. In contrast, the practice of considering environmental and social factors has been slower to take hold.

6. A is correct. A specific concern among investors of energy companies is the existence of "stranded assets," which are carbon-intensive assets at risk of no longer being economically viable because of changes in regulation or investor sentiment.

7. C is correct. Material environmental effects can arise from strategic or operational decisions based on inadequate governance processes or errors in judgment. For example, oil spills, industrial waste contamination events, and local resource depletion can result from poor environmental standards, breaches in safety standards, or unsustainable business models. Such events can be costly in terms of regulatory fines, litigation, clean-up costs, reputational risk, and resource management.

8. C is correct. *Responsible investing* is the broadest (umbrella) term used to describe investment strategies that incorporate environmental, social, and governance (ESG) factors into their approaches.

9. A is correct. Social factors considered in ESG implementation generally pertain to the management of the human capital of a business, including data privacy and security.

10. A is correct. Negative screening refers to the practice of excluding certain sectors, companies, or practices that do not meet specific ESG criteria based on the investor's values, ethics, or preferences.

11. B is correct. While leverage increases risk for all stakeholders, shareholders generally benefit through higher potential returns. Senior management typically benefits through equity-based compensation. For non-management employees, equity-based compensation is likely to be small to non-existent.

12. C is correct. Corporate governance is the arrangement of checks, balances, and incentives a company needs to minimize and manage the conflicting interests between insiders and external shareholders.

13. B is correct. The board typically ensures that the company has an appropriate enterprise risk management system in place.

14. B is correct. A common law system offers better protection of shareholder interests than does a civil law system.

CHAPTER 3

WORKING CAPITAL & LIQUIDITY

SOLUTIONS

1. C is correct. Although accounts payable do not charge an explicit interest rate, the cost of accounts payable is reflected in the costs of the services or products purchased and in the costs of any discounts not taken. Accounts payable can have a very high implicit cost. Similarly, equity financing is not free. A required return is expected on shareholder financing just as on any other form of financing.

2. C is correct. A revolver is a short-term borrowing facility in which a bank allows the firm to borrow and repay loans during the life of the line of credit.

3. A is correct. SOA must issue 19 million of bonds.

Source	Amount (local, millions)
Accounts payable	6
Bank loan against receivables	8
Short-term note	14
Net income + depreciation – dividends	28
Total sources	56

   The firm requires 75 million of financing in local currency terms. Given that the planned sources (before bond financing or repurchases) total 56 million, SOA will need to issue 19 million of new bonds.

4. C is correct. In a moderate approach, XY1 would attempt to match the duration of the assets with the liabilities. This would allow the company to use long-term financing for permanent working capital needs while at the same time looking to minimize interest expense through the use of more flexible short-term financing on an as-needed basis.

5. C is correct. Kwam must sell the entire real estate property because the two primary sources (marketable securities and bonds) will not raise the needed €120 million. A is incorrect because it assumes a fractional real estate sale. The real estate sale will raise a net of €63 million (€70 million minus 10% liquidation expenses). To raise the rest of the funds needed (€120 million – €63 million = €57 million), Kwam can sell €57 million of marketable securities, which have minimal liquidation/brokerage costs.

6. C is correct. A longer average collection period will certainly occur. Higher cash balances and a lower level of uncollectible accounts will not occur.

7. B is correct. Reducing the average collection period would speed up receipts and improve the firm's liquidity position. The other two suggestions would worsen the firm's liquidity position.

8. A is correct. Relative to peers, Company H has the highest set of ratios. Relative to historical average ratios, Company H's recent ratios show the greatest increases. The cash ratio is the most relevant for judging liquidity, and Company H's cash ratio is quite high.

9. C is correct. Company S's cash conversion cycle nearly doubled over recent years, while the cash conversion cycles for Companies H and J are nearly unchanged. The days of inventory on hand and days of receivables both increased substantially for Company S, and its days of payables outstanding decreased very slightly. The net effect was the large increase in the cash conversion cycle. Although changes occurred in the components of the cash conversion cycles for Companies H and J, the net effect on their cash conversion cycles was small.

10. C is correct. Accounts payable and accruals are internal and a source of cash as they are payments not yet made to suppliers, employees, or other related parties. Lines of credit are external sources of financing. Accounts receivable and inventory are internal uses of cash since a company must access financing to purchase inventory and lend to its customers.

CHAPTER 4

CAPITAL INVESTMENTS

SOLUTIONS

1. B is correct. Costs to finance the investment are taken into account when the cash flows are discounted at the appropriate COC; including interest costs in the cash flows would result in double-counting the cost of debt.

2. C is correct. The NPV sums the investment's expected cash flows (CF) discounted at the opportunity COC. The NPV calculation is

$$NPV = \sum_{t=0}^{N} \frac{CF_t}{(1+r)^t},$$

    where
    CF_t = the expected net cash flow at time t
    N = the investment's projected life
    r = the discount rate or opportunity COC

3. A is correct.

$$NPV = -\$2.2 + \frac{\$1.3}{(1.08)} + \frac{\$1.6}{(1.08)^2} + \frac{\$1.9}{(1.08)^3} + \frac{\$0.8}{(1.08)^4} = \$2.47 \text{ million.}$$

4. C is correct. The IRR is computed by identifying all cash flows and solving for the rate that makes the NPV of those cash flows equal to zero.

5. B is correct. Using either the IRR function in Excel or a financial calculator, IRR is determined by setting the NPV equal to zero for the cash flows shown in the following table.

Year	0	1	2	3
Cash flow (GBP)	−1,000	200	200	900

6. C is correct.

$$NPV = -50,000 + \frac{15,000}{1.08} + \frac{15,000}{1.08^2} + \frac{20,000}{1.08^3} + \frac{10,000}{1.08^4} + \frac{5,000}{1.08^5}.$$

$$NPV = -50,000 + 13,888.89 + 12,860.08 + 15,876.64 + 7,350.30 + 3,402.92.$$

$$NPV = -50,000 + 53,378.83 = 3,378.83.$$

   Using either the IRR function in Excel or a financial calculator, the IRR is 10.88%.

7. B is correct.

$$NPV = \sum_{t=0}^{3} \frac{CF_t}{(1+r)^t} = -100 + \frac{40}{1.20} + \frac{80}{1.20^2} + \frac{120}{1.20^3} = \$58.33.$$

8. C is correct. Using a financial calculator or the trial-and-error method, the IRR is 28.79%. The COC, which is stated as 10%, is not used to solve the problem.

		Present Value			
Year	Cash Flow	28.19%	28.39%	28.59%	28.79%
0	−150,000	−150,000	−150,000	−150,000	−150,000
1	100,000	78,009	77,888	77,767	77,646
2	120,000	73,025	72,798	72,572	72,346
Total		1,034	686	338	−8

Year	0	1	2
Cash flow	−150,000	100,000	120,000

   Using the IRR function in Excel results in a more precise IRR of 28.7854% with a total present value closer to zero.

9. A is correct.

$$NPV = -750 + \sum_{t=1}^{7} \frac{175}{1.10^t} = -750 + 851.97 = 101.97 \text{ million won.}$$

   Using either the IRR function in Excel or a financial calculator, the IRR is 14.02%. Using a financial calculator, present value is −750, $N = 7$, and PMT = 175.

10. B is correct. The IRR would stay the same because both the initial outlay and the after-tax cash flows double, so the return on each dollar invested would remain the same. All the cash flows and their present values double. The difference between the total present value of the future cash flows and the initial outlay (the NPV) also doubles.

11. C is correct. There are many factors that can affect the stock price, including whether Ms. Ndereba's analysis indicates that the project is more or less profitable than investors expected.

12. A is correct. Because all Bearing's projects have a positive NPV, they are all providing a return that is greater than the opportunity COC. Therefore, the ROIC must be greater than the COC.

13. C is correct. When valuing mutually exclusive investments, the decision should be made with the NPV method because this method uses the most realistic discount rate—namely, the opportunity cost of funds. In this example, the reinvestment rate for the NPV method (here, 10%) is more realistic than the reinvestment rate for the IRR method (here, 21.86% or 18.92%).

14. B is correct. For these investments, a discount rate of 13.16% would yield the same NPV for both (an NPV of 6.73).

15. C is correct. Discount rates of 0% and approximately 61.8% both give an NPV of zero.

Rate	0%	20%	40%	60%	61.8%	80%	100%
NPV	0.00	4.40	3.21	0.29	0.00	−3.02	−6.25

16. C is correct. Expansion projects increase the scale of a firm's existing activities and/or extend a firm's reach into new product or service categories and markets, in the hopes of generating longer-term expected gains. Regulatory/compliance projects are required for the business to continue operations but otherwise might not be undertaken by a company. Going concern projects benefit the company through improved efficiencies and cost savings over time.

17. B is correct.

    If demand is "high," the NPV is as follows:

    $$NPV = -190 + \sum_{t=1}^{10} \frac{40}{1.10^t} = C\$55.78 \text{ million.}$$

    If demand is "low," the NPV is

    $$NPV = -190 + \sum_{t=1}^{10} \frac{20}{1.10^t} = -C\$67.11 \text{ million.}$$

    The expected NPV is 0.50(55.78) + 0.50(–67.11) = –C\$5.66 million.

18. B is correct. The additional NPV of adding shifts if demand is "high" is

    $$NPV = \sum_{t=2}^{10} \frac{5}{1.10^t} = C\$26.18 \text{ million.}$$

    If demand is "low," the production-flexibility option will not be exercised. The optimal decision is to add shifts only if demand is high.

    Because the production-flexibility option is exercised only when demand is high, which happens 50% of the time, the expected present value of adding shifts is

$$NPV = 0.50(26.18) = CAD3.09 \text{ million.}$$

The total NPV of the initial project and the production-flexibility option is

$$NPV = -CAD5.66 \text{ million} + CAD13.09 \text{ million} = CAD7.43 \text{ million.}$$

The option to add shifts, handled optimally, adds sufficient value to make this a positive-NPV project.

19. B is correct. In valuing investments, expected cash flows should be discounted at required rates of return that reflect their risk, not at a risk-free rate that ignores risk. NPV is superior to IRR. Choosing projects based on IRR might cause the company to concentrate on short-term investments that do not maximize the company's NPV.

CHAPTER 5

CAPITAL STRUCTURE

SOLUTIONS

1. C is correct. Stock dividends, like stock splits, have no impact on the value of a company's equity. Issuing shares to acquire a competitor would increase equity relative to debt in the capital structure. Share price appreciation would also increase the market value of equity, thus increasing equity relative to debt.

2. C is correct. For a start-up company of this nature, debt financing is likely to be unattractive to lenders—and therefore very expensive or difficult to obtain. Debt financing is also unappealing to the company, because it commits the company to interest and principal payments that might be difficult to manage given the company's uncertain cash flow outlook.

3. B is correct. Cash flow typically turns positive during the growth stage, but it may be negative, particularly at the beginning of this stage.

4. C is correct. An electric utility has the capacity to support substantial debt, with very stable and predictable revenues and cash flows. The software company also has these attributes, but it would have been much less likely to have raised debt during its development and may have raised equity. The mining company has fixed assets, which it would have needed to finance, but the cyclical nature of its business would limit its debt capacity.

5. C is correct. As cash flows become more predictable, the company is able to support more debt in its capital structure; the optimal capital structure includes a higher proportion of debt. While mature companies do borrow to support growth, this action would typically not occur because the company is optimizing its capital structure. Likewise, while a mature company might issue equity to finance growth, this action would not be the typical approach for a company optimizing its capital structure.

6. B is correct. Proposition I, or the capital structure irrelevance theorem, states that in perfect markets the level of debt versus equity in the capital structure has no effect on company value.

7. C is correct. The cost of equity rises with the use of debt in the capital structure (e.g., with increasing financial leverage).

8. C is correct. If the company's WACC increases as a result of taking on additional debt, the company has moved beyond the optimal capital range. The costs of financial distress may outweigh any tax benefits from the use of debt.

9. B is correct. The static trade-off theory indicates that there is a trade-off between the tax shield for interest on debt and the costs of financial distress, leading to an optimal amount of debt in a company's capital structure.

10. A is correct. The market value of equity is (USD30)(10,000,000) = USD300,000,000. With the market value of debt equal to USD100,000,000, the market value of the company is USD100,000,000 + USD300,000,000 = USD400,000,000. Therefore, the company is USD100,000,000/USD400,000,000 = 0.25, or 25% debt-financed.

11. A is correct. The after-tax cost of debt decreases as the marginal tax rate increases.

12. B is correct. A company's optimal and target capital structures may be different from each other.

13. C is correct. Long-term debt is more exposed than short-term debt to the risk of a management decision that is not debtholder-friendly. Secured debt is less exposed than unsecured debt to such a risk, and with low leverage, the risk of a debt-equity conflict is reduced, not increased, relative to high leverage.

14. B is correct. Management is advocating an acquisition that is likely to be positive for the value of the company's options but negative for equityholders, given the substantial risk. A is an example of a debt-equity conflict. C is an example of stakeholder interests that are not being considered by management.

15. B is correct. Management is generally focused on maximizing the value of equity.

16. B is correct. A well-designed management compensation scheme can reduce, but not eliminate, agency costs.

17. The cyclical nature of ISS's revenues, which cause the company's earnings and cash flows to vary considerably over the business cycle, would point to a relatively high cost of borrowing and low proportion of debt in the capital structure. Revenue and earnings streams subject to relatively high volatility, and consequently less predictability, are less favorable for supporting debt in the capital structure. Further, companies with pay-per-use business models, rather than subscription-based models, are likely to have a lower degree of revenue predictability and a lower ability to support debt in the capital structure.

   Another factor pointing to a relatively high cost of borrowing and low proportion of debt in the capital structure is the fact that most of the company's assets are intangible and thus less likely to be accepted by lenders as collateral for secured financing. Asset-light companies with a lower proportion of tangible assets will have a lower ability to support debt in the capital structure.

18. The fact that Tillett earns about half of its revenues from subscription-based service agreements would suggest that the company's revenue stream is likely somewhat predictable. A high proportion of recurring revenues for a company is generally viewed as a positive for its ability to support debt, because the company's revenue stream is likely to be more predictable and less sensitive to the ups and downs of the macro economy. Further, Tillett's assets consist mostly of inventory and property, plant, and equipment, representing its production facilities. Tangible assets, such as inventory and property, plant, and equipment, are often deemed safer than intangible assets and can better serve as debt collateral. Finally, the fact that Tillett currently has no debt in its capital structure and has experienced improved profitability in recent years would also suggest that Tillett might be able to access debt capital at a reasonable cost to finance the additional growth.

19. Leverage ratios and interest coverage ratios are commonly used to determine whether a company can service additional debt. Regarding leverage ratios, a company's ratio of total debt to total assets measures the proportion of total assets funded by debt capital, and its ratio of total debt to EBITDA provides an estimate of how many years it would take to repay its total debt based on EBITDA (a proxy for operating cash flow). The interest

coverage ratio (EBIT to interest expense) measures the number of times a company's EBIT could cover its interest payments.

20. A company's cost of debt is equal to a risk-free rate plus a credit spread specific to the company. Lower interest rates and tighter credit spreads would make borrowing less costly and make debt financing relatively more attractive than when interest rates are high or credit spreads are wide.

21. C is correct. Share price changes will cause the market value of the company's equity to change; book value is unaffected.

    Statements A and B are accurate.

22. C is correct.

$$w_d = \text{USD}63/(\text{USD}220 + \text{USD}63) = 0.223.$$
$$w_e = \text{USD}220/(\text{USD}220 + \text{USD}63) = 0.777.$$

Market values should be used in cost of capital calculations, and forecasted market values should be used in this case given that the cost of capital will be applied to *projected* cash flows in McClure's analysis.

23. C is correct. Companies generally raise capital when it is needed, such as for investment spending or when market pricing and terms are favorable for debt or equity issuance.

24. A is correct. According to the pecking order theory, internally generated funds are preferable to both new equity and new debt. If internal financing is insufficient, managers next prefer new debt, then new equity. Managers prefer forms of financing with the least amount of visibility to outsiders.

25. C is correct. According to the pecking order theory, managers prefer internal financing. If internal financing is insufficient, managers next prefer debt, then equity—in order of increasing visibility to outsiders.

CHAPTER 6

MEASURES OF LEVERAGE

SOLUTIONS

1. C is correct. Sales risk is defined as uncertainty with respect to the price or quantity of goods and services sold. 4G has a higher standard deviation of unit sales than Qphone; in addition, 4G's standard deviation of unit sales stated as a fraction of its level of unit sales, at $25,000/1,000,000 = 0.025$, is greater than the comparable ratio for Qphone, $10,000/1,500,000 = 0.0067$.

2. B is correct. Business risk is associated with operating earnings. Operating earnings are affected by sales risk (uncertainty with respect to price and quantity), and operating risk (the operating cost structure and the level of fixed costs).

3. C is correct. Operating risk refers to the risk arising from the mix of fixed and variable costs.

4. B is correct. $\text{DOL} = \frac{Q(P-V)}{Q(P-V)-F}$

$$\text{DOL @ } 1,000,000 \text{ units} = \frac{1,000,000(¥108 - ¥72)}{1,000,000(¥108 - ¥72) - ¥22,500,000} = 2.67$$

5. C is correct. Degree of financial leverage is

$$\text{DFL} = \frac{[Q(P-V)-F]}{[Q(P-V)-F-C]}$$
$$= \frac{1,000,000(¥108 - ¥72) - ¥22,500,000}{1,000,000(¥108 - ¥72) - ¥22,500,000 - ¥9,000,000} = 3.00$$

6. B is correct. The degree of operating leverage of Qphone is 1.4. The percentage change in operating income is equal to the DOL times the percentage change in units sold, therefore:

$$\text{Percentage change in operating income} = (\text{DOL})\left(\text{Percentage change in units sold}\right) = (1.4)(15\%) = 21\%$$

7. C is correct. The breakeven quantity is computed

$$Q_{BE} = \frac{F+C}{P-V} = \frac{(¥22,500,000 + ¥9,000,000)}{(¥108 - ¥72)} = 875,000$$

8. C is correct. 4G, Inc.'s degree of total leverage can be shown to equal 8, whereas Qphone Corp.'s degree of total leverage is only DOL × DFL = 1.4 × 1.15 = 1.61. Therefore, a 10 percent increase in unit sales will mean an 80 percent increase in net income for 4G, but only a 16.1 percent increase in net income for Qphone Corp. The calculation for 4G, Inc.'s DTL is

$$\text{DTL} = \frac{Q(P-V)}{Q(P-V) - F - C}$$

$$= \frac{1,000,000(¥108 - ¥72)}{1,000,000(¥108 - ¥72) - ¥22,500,000 - ¥9,000,000} = 8.00$$

9. A is correct. Degree of total leverage is defined as the percentage change in net income divided by the percentage change in units sold.
10. C is correct. The companies' degree of operating leverage should be the same, consistent with C. Sales risk refers to the uncertainty of the number of units produced and sold and the price at which units are sold. Business risk is the joint effect of sales risk and operating risk.
11. C is correct. The degree of operating leverage is the elasticity of operating earnings with respect to the number of units produced and sold. As an elasticity, the degree of operating leverage measures the sensitivity of operating earnings to a change in the number of units produced and sold.
12. C is correct. Because DOL is 4, if unit sales increase by 5 percent, Fulcrum's operating earnings are expected to increase by 4 × 5% = 20%. The calculation for DOL is:

$$\text{DOL} = \frac{(40 \text{ million})(\$100 - \$65)}{[(40 \text{ million})(\$100 - \$65)] - \$1.05 \text{ billion}}$$

$$= \frac{\$1.400 \text{ billion}}{\$1.400 \text{ billion} - \$1.05 \text{ billion}} = \frac{\$1.4}{\$0.35} = 4$$

13. C is correct. Business risk reflects operating leverage and factors that affect sales (such as those given).
14. B is correct. Grundlegend's degree of operating leverage is the same as Basic Company's, whereas Grundlegend's degree of total leverage and degree of financial leverage are higher.
15. B is correct.

$$\text{Operating breakeven units} = \frac{¥1,290 \text{ million}}{(¥3,529 - ¥1,500)} = 635,781.173 \text{ units}$$

$$\text{Operating breakeven sales} = ¥3,529 \times 635,781.173 \text{ units} = ¥2,243,671,760$$

or

$$\text{Operating breakeven sales} = \frac{¥1,290 \text{ million}}{1 - (¥1,500/¥3,529)} = ¥2,243,671,760$$

$$\text{Total breakeven} = \frac{\yen 1{,}290 \text{ million} + \yen 410 \text{ million}}{(\yen 3{,}529 - \yen 1{,}500)} = \frac{\yen 1{,}700 \text{ million}}{\yen 2{,}029}$$

$$= 837{,}851.1582 \text{ units}$$

$$\text{Breakeven sales} = \yen 3{,}529 \times 837{,}851.1582 \text{ units} = \yen 2{,}956{,}776{,}737$$

or

$$\text{Breakeven sales} = \frac{\yen 1{,}700 \text{ million}}{1 - (\yen 1{,}500 / \yen 3{,}529)} = \yen 2{,}956{,}776{,}737$$

16. A is correct. For The Gearing Company,

$$Q_{\text{BE}} = \frac{F + C}{P - V} = \frac{\$40 \text{ million} + \$20 \text{ million}}{\$200 - \$120} = 750{,}000$$

For Hebelkraft, Inc.,

$$Q_{\text{BE}} = \frac{F + C}{P - V} = \frac{\$90 \text{ million} + \$20 \text{ million}}{\$200 - \$100} = 1{,}100{,}000$$

COST OF CAPITAL: FOUNDATIONAL TOPICS

SOLUTIONS

1. B is correct.

$$r_e = 0.0425 + (1.3)(0.0482) = 0.1052, \text{ or } 10.52\%.$$

2. B is correct.

$$\text{WACC} = [(\text{€}900/\text{€}3300)(0.0925)(1 - 0.375)] + [(\text{€}2,400/\text{€}3,300)(0.1052)]$$
$$= 0.0923, \text{ or } 9.23\%.$$

3. A is correct.

Asset beta = Unlevered beta = $1.3/\{1 + [(1 - 0.375)(\text{€}900/\text{€}2,400)]\} = 1.053$.

4. C is correct.

Project beta = $1.053\{1 + [(1 - 0.375)(\text{€}80/\text{€}20)]\} = 1.053(3.5) = 3.686$.

5. C is correct.

$$r_e = 0.0425 + 3.686(0.0482 + 0.0188) = 0.2895, \text{ or } 28.95\%.$$

6. B is correct. Debt is generally less costly than preferred or common stock. The cost of debt is further reduced if interest expense is tax deductible.
7. B is correct. The weighted average cost of capital, using weights derived from the current capital structure, is the best estimate of the cost of capital for the average-risk project of a company.
8. C is correct. McClure should use the forecasted or target market values to calculate the weights.

$$w_d = \$63/(\$220 + 63) = 0.223.$$

$$w_e = \$220/(\$220 + 63) = 0.777.$$

9. The company's WACC is 13.64%, calculated as follows:

	Equity	Debt	WACC
Weight	0.80	0.20	
After-Tax Cost	15.6%	(1 − 0.30)8.28%	
Weight × Cost	12.48%	+ 1.16%	= 13.64%

10. B is correct. The cost of equity is defined as the rate of return required by stockholders.

11. C is correct. $FV = \$1,000$, $PMT = \$40$, $N = 10$, and $PV = \$900$.

$$\text{Solve for } i. \text{ The six-month yield, } i, \text{ is } 5.3149\%.$$

$$YTM = 5.3149\% \times 2 = 10.62985\%.$$

$$r_d(1 - t) = 10.62985\%(1 - 0.38) = 6.5905\%.$$

12. C is correct. The bond rating approach depends on knowledge of the company's rating and can be compared with yields on bonds in the public market.

13. B is correct. The company can issue preferred stock at 6.5%. Therefore, the calculation of the preferred stock's current value is

$$P_p = \$1.75/0.065 = \$26.92.$$

14. A is correct. The relevant cost is the marginal cost of debt. The before-tax marginal cost of debt can be estimated by the yield to maturity of the company's expected new issue, which is 7%. After adjusting for tax, the after-tax cost is $7\%(1 - 0.4) = 7\%(0.6) = 4.2\%$.

15. For JPMorgan Chase, the required return is

$$r = R_F + \beta[E(R_M) - R_F] = 4.35\% + 1.50(8.04\%) = 4.35\% + 12.06\%$$

$$= 16.41\%.$$

For Boeing, the required return is

$$r = R_F + \beta[E(R_M) - R_F] = 4.35\% + 0.80(8.04\%) = 4.35\% + 6.43\%$$

$$= 10.78\%.$$

16. A. The required return is given by

$$r = 0.025 + (-0.2)(0.045) = 2.5\% - 0.9\% = 1.6\%.$$

This example indicates that Newmont Mining has a required return of 1.6%. When beta is negative, the CAPM calculation yields a required rate of return that is below the risk-free rate, which is arguably not meaningful. Cases of equities with negative betas are relatively rare.

B. The fact that the NEM's cost of debt is higher than the calculated required return on equity is another indicator that the return estimated using CAPM is not useful for valuing the company's equity.

17. B is correct. Asset risk does not change with a higher debt-to-equity ratio. Equity risk rises with higher debt.

18. B is correct. The debt-to-equity ratio of the new product should be used when making the adjustment from the asset beta, derived from the comparables, to the equity beta of the new product.

19. B is correct. The capital structure is as follows:

Market value of debt: $FV = \$10,000,000$, $PMT = \$400,000$, $N = 10$, and $I/YR = 6.825\%$. Solving for *PV* gives $7,999,688.
Market value of equity: 1.2 million shares outstanding at $10 = \$12,000,000$.

Market value of debt	$7,999,688	40%
Market value of equity	12,000,000	60%
Total capital	$19,999,688	100%

To raise $7.5 million of new capital while maintaining the same capital structure, the company would issue $7.5 million × 40% = $3.0 million in bonds, which results in a before-tax rate of 16%.

$$r_d(1 - t) = 0.16(1 - 0.3) = 0.112, \text{ or } 11.2\%.$$

$$r_e = 0.03 + 2.2(0.10 - 0.03) = 0.184, \text{ or } 18.4\%.$$

$$\text{WACC} = 0.40(0.112) + 0.6(0.184) = 0.0448 + 0.1104 = 0.1552, \text{ or } 15.52\%.$$

20. B is correct.

$$\text{Asset beta: } \beta_{equity}/[1 + (1 - t)(D/E)]$$

$$\text{Relevant} = 1.702/[1 + (0.77)(0)] = 1.702.$$

$$\text{ABJ} = 2.8/[1 + (0.77)(0.003)] = 2.7918.$$

$$\text{Opus} = 3.4/[1 + (0.77)(0.013)] = 3.3663.$$

21. C is correct.
Weights are determined on the basis of relative market values:

Comparables	Market Value of Equity in Millions	Proportion of Total
Relevant	$3,800	0.5490
ABJ	2,150	0.3106
Opus	972	0.1404
Total	$6,922	1.0000

Weighted average beta = $(0.5490)(1.702) + (0.3106)(2.7918) + (0.1404)(3.3572) = 2.27$.

22. B is correct.

$$\text{Asset beta} = 2.27.$$

$$\text{Levered beta} = 2.27[1 + (1 - 0.23)(0.01)] = 2.2875.$$

$$\text{Cost of equity capital} = 0.0525 + (2.2875)(0.07) = 0.2126, \text{ or } 21.26\%.$$

23. C is correct.

For debt: $FV = 2,400,000$; $PV = 2,156,000$; $n = 10$; $PMT = 150,000$.

Solve for i: $i = 0.07748$. YTM = 15.5%.

Before-tax cost of debt = 15.5%.

Market value of equity = 1 million shares outstanding + 1 million newly issued shares = 2 million shares at $8 = $16 million.

Total market capitalization = $2.156 million + $16 million = $18.156 million.

Levered beta = $2.27[1 + (1 - 0.23)(2.156/16)] = 2.27(1.1038) = 2.5055.$

Cost of equity = $0.0525 + 2.5055(0.07) = 0.2279$, or 22.79%.

Debt weight = $2.156/$18.156 = 0.1187.

Equity weight = $16/$18.156 = 0.8813.

$$\text{TagOn's MCC} = (0.1187)(0.155)(1 - 0.23) + (0.8813)(0.2279)$$

$$= 0.01417 + 0.20084$$

$$= 0.2150. \text{ or } 21.50\%.$$

24. C is correct. Inferring the asset beta for the public company: Unlevered beta = $1.75/[1 + (1 - 0.35)(0.90)] = 1.104$. Re-levering to reflect the target debt ratio of the private firm: Levered beta = $1.104 \times [1 + (1 - 0.30)(1.00)] = 1.877$.

25. B is correct. All else equal, the first issue's greater liquidity would tend to make its required return lower than the second issue's. However, the required return on equity increases as leverage increases. The first issue's higher required return must result from its higher leverage, more than offsetting the effect of its greater liquidity, given that both issues have the same market risk.

26. B is correct. Since the project will be financed with 50% equity, the company will issue £25 million of new stock. The flotation cost of external equity is $(0.058 \times 25,000,000) = 1,450,000$. The NPV of the project using external equity is the NPV using internal equity less the flotation cost. Adjusting the cost of capital to reflect the flotation cost is not a preferred way to account for flotation costs.

CHAPTER 8

COST OF CAPITAL: ADVANCED TOPICS

SOLUTIONS

1. LM estimates the cost of debt for Precision by estimating a synthetic yield on the company's 10-year bonds. Given the information in Panel B of Exhibit 16, Precision's IC ratio is 7.63 (= 12.2/1.6), and its D/E ratio is 0.2120 (= 18.4/(105.2 − 18.4)). Given the synthetic rating schedule in Exhibit 17, these leverage ratios imply a synthetic credit rating of A and an implied credit spread of 1.46%.
   Adding this credit spread and the CRP of 2% to the 10-year benchmark government bond yield of 5.41% yields a cost of debt estimate of

   $$5.41\% + 1.46\% + 2.00\% = 8.87\%.$$

   The after-tax cost of debt is then estimated at 8.87% (1 − 0.20) = 7.096%.

2. LM estimates a SP of 5% for Precision (Exhibit 18). This is likely driven by the company's relatively small size compared to the industry. As shown in Exhibit 16, as measured by total assets, Precision (105.2 million) is less than 1/10 the size of the average publicly traded company in the industry (1.276 billion). Given that the SP is typically assumed to be inversely related to company size, it seems reasonable that LM chose an SP near the high end of the range used by the corporate development group.

3. Company characteristics that would justify a higher SCRP for Precision would be

   - a lower proportion of assets that are tangible and liquid compared to the industry,
   - high customer concentration risk,
   - high geographic concentration risk, and
   - significant key person risk.

   First, compared to the industry average, Precision has an asset base that consists of a significant amount of intangible assets (47% versus 32%), and the company also holds less cash and equivalents (9% versus 14%). All else equal, companies with asset bases comprising relatively high proportions of intangible and illiquid assets are more likely to have higher costs of equity.
   Second, Precision has significant customer and geographic concentration risk, as evidenced by the fact that approximately 70% of revenues come from five major customers within close geographic proximity of each other. Finally, the founder and

CEO appears to be involved in all aspects of the business, with no clear succession plan in place, which points to significant key-person risk.

Company characteristics that would justify a lower SCRP for Precision would be:

- a higher proportion of recurring revenues and
- lower financial leverage in comparison to the industry.

First, approximately 60% of the company's revenues come from software subscriptions, which suggests a high proportion of recurring revenues. Companies with a high proportion of recurring revenues typically have lower costs of equity because these companies have relatively more stable earnings and cash flow streams.

Second, Precision is operating with less leverage than the mean software company, as evidenced by a lower D/E ratio of 0.2120, versus the industry average of 0.3025 (= 296.4/(1,276.2 − 296.4)), and a slightly higher IC ratio of 7.63, versus 7.55 for the industry (= 177.4/23.5).

4. Precision's estimated cost of common equity using the extended CAPM is 26.56%, calculated as

$$r_e = r_f + \beta(\text{ERP}) + \text{SP} + \text{IP} + \text{SCP}.$$

The first step is to estimate a beta for Precision. To do so, start by unlevering the industry beta to arrive at an asset beta using the marginal tax rate of 20% and D/E ratio of 0.3025:

$$\beta_{Asset} = \beta_c \left[\frac{1}{1 + \left((1 - t_c) \frac{D_c}{E_c} \right)} \right]$$

$$\beta_{Asset} = 1.25 \left[\frac{1}{(1 + (1 - 0.25)(0.3025))} \right] = 1.019.$$

The second step is to compute the estimated beta for Precision given its marginal tax rate and D/E ratio:

$$\beta_{Precision} = \beta_{Asset} \left[1 + \left((1 - t_S) \frac{D_S}{E_S} \right) \right]$$

$$\beta_{Precision} = 1.019[1 + ((1 - 0.20)0.2120)] = 1.19.$$

Finally, calculate the cost of equity using the estimated beta for Precision, the risk premiums from Exhibit 18, and the additional CRP of 2%:

$$r_e = 5.41\% + 1.19(6\%) + 5\% + 1\% + 6\% + 2\% = 26.55\%.$$

Precision's estimated cost of common equity using the build-up approach, inclusive of the additional CRP of 2%, is 25.41%, calculated as

$$r_e = r_f + \text{ERP} + \text{SP} + \text{SCRP} + \text{CRP}$$

$$r_e = 5.41\% + 6\% + 5\% + 6\% + 2\% = 24.41\%.$$

5. Precision's estimated WACC is 21.13%, calculated as

$$r_{wacc} = w_d r_d (1 - t) + w_e r_e$$

$$r_{wacc} = (0.1749)(0.07096)(1 - 0.20) + (0.8251)(0.2441) = 0.2113, \text{ or } 21.13\%$$

where

$$w_d = 18.4/105.2 = 0.1749$$

$$w_e = (105.2 - 18.4)/105.2 = 0.8251$$

6. A is correct. The backfilling of index returns using companies that have survived to the index construction date is expected to introduce a positive survivorship bias into returns.

7. B is correct. The events of Year 12 through Year 16 depressed share returns but (1) are not a persistent feature of the stock market environment, (2) were not offset by other positive events within the historical record, and (3) have led to relatively low valuation levels, which are expected to rebound.

8. A is correct. The required return reflects the magnitude of the historical ERP, which is generally higher when based on a short-term interest rate (as a result of the normal upward-sloping yield curve), and the current value of the rate being used to represent the risk-free rate. The short-term rate is currently higher than the long-term rate, which will also increase the required return estimate. The short-term interest rate, however, overstates the long-term expected inflation rate. Using the short-term interest rate, estimates of the long-term required return on equity will be biased upward.

9. B is correct.

$$i = 4\% \text{ per year (long-term forecast of inflation)}$$

$$g = 4\% \text{ per year (growth in real GDP)}$$

$$\Delta \text{ (P/E0} = 1\% \text{ per year (growth in market P/E)}$$

$$dy = 1\% \text{ per year (dividend yield or the income portion)}$$

$$\text{Risk-free return} = r_f = 7\% \text{ per year (for 10-year maturities)}$$

Using the Grinold-Kroner model, the ERP estimate is

$$ERP = \{1.0 + 1.0 + [4.0 + 4.0 + 0.0)]\} - 7.0 = 3.0\%.$$

The premium of 3.0% compensates investors for average market risk, given expectations for inflation, real earnings growth, P/E growth, and anticipated income.

10. C is correct. Based on a long-term government bond yield of 7%, a beta of 1, and any of the risk premium estimates that can be calculated from the givens (e.g., a 2% historical risk premium estimate or 3.0% Grinold-Kroner ERP estimate), the required rate of return would be at least 9%. Based on using a short-term rate of 9%, C is the correct choice.

CHAPTER **9**

ANALYSIS OF DIVIDENDS AND SHARE REPURCHASES

SOLUTIONS

1. C is correct. A stock dividend is accounted for as a transfer of retained earnings to contributed capital.
2. C is correct. A reverse stock split would increase the price per share of the stock to a higher, more marketable range that could possibly increase the number of investors who would consider buying the stock.
3. A is correct. Both statements are incorrect. A stock dividend will decrease the price per share, all other things being equal. A stock split will reduce the price and earnings per share proportionately, leaving the price-to-earnings ratio the same.
4. A is correct. By reducing corporate cash, a cash dividend reduces the current ratio, whereas a stock dividend (whatever the size) has no effect on the current ratio.
5. C is correct. The implementation of Proposal #1, a stock dividend, would not affect a shareholder's proportionate ownership because all shareholders would receive the same proportionate increase in shares. Stock dividends, which are generally not taxable to shareholders, do not impact an investor's total cost basis (they merely reduce the cost basis per share).

   A is incorrect because stock dividends are generally not taxable to shareholders. A stock dividend merely divides the "pie" (the market value of shareholders' equity) into smaller pieces.

   B is incorrect because an investor's total cost basis will not be affected by a stock dividend; a stock dividend merely reduces the cost basis per share.
6. B is correct. If Yeta implemented Proposal #2, a repurchase of US$40 million in shares, the resulting book value per share (BVPS) would be US$25.71, calculated as follows:

   1. Yeta has a current BVPS of US$25.60; therefore, total book value of equity is US$2,560 million (= US$25.60 × 100,000,000 shares).
   2. The number of shares Yeta would repurchase is US$40 million/US$20.00 per share = 2 million shares.
   3. Yeta shareholders' book value of equity after the buyback would be US$2,520 million (= US$2,560 million – US$40 million).
   4. The number of shares after the buyback would be 98 million (= 100 million – 2 million).
   5. The BVPS after the buyback would be US$2,520 million/98 million = US$25.71.

A is incorrect because US$25.20 incorrectly uses 100 million shares instead of 98 million shares in calculating BVPS after the buyback: US$2,520 million/100 million = US$25.20.

C is incorrect because US$26.12 incorrectly uses US$2,560 million (current book value) instead of US$2,520 million as the book value of equity in calculating BVPS after the buyback. The BVPS after the buyback is incorrectly calculated as US$2,560 million/ 98 million = US$26.12.

7. C is correct. In the case of external funding, a company's earnings per share will increase if the stock's earnings yield, which is the ratio of earnings per share to share price, exceeds the after-tax cost of borrowing. Yeta's earnings yield is 9.10% (= US$1.82/US$20.00), which exceeds the after-tax cost of borrowing of 8.50%.

A is incorrect because EPS will increase (not decrease) if the stock's earnings yield (= US$1.82/US$20.00) exceeds the after-tax cost of borrowing. Yeta's earnings yield of 9.10% exceeds the after-tax cost of borrowing of 8.50%.

B is incorrect because EPS will increase (not remain unchanged) if the stock's earnings yield (= US$1.82/US$20.00) exceeds the after-tax cost of borrowing. Yeta's earnings yield of 9.10% exceeds the after-tax cost of borrowing of 8.50%.

8. A is correct. Yeta is financed by both debt and equity; therefore, paying dividends can increase the agency conflict between shareholders and bondholders. The payment of dividends reduces the cash cushion available for the disbursement of fixed required payments to bondholders. All else equal, dividends increase the default risk of debt.

B is incorrect because the agency conflict between shareholders and managers would decrease (not increase) with the payment of dividends. Paying out free cash flow to equity in dividends would constrain managers in their ability to overinvest by taking on negative net present value (NPV) projects.

C is incorrect because paying dividends can increase (not decrease) the agency conflict between shareholders and bondholders. The payment of dividends would reduce the cash cushion available to Yeta for the disbursement of fixed required payments to bondholders. The payment of dividends transfers wealth from bondholders to shareholders and increases the default risk of debt.

9. C is correct. Dividend initiations convey positive information and are associated with future earnings growth, whereas dividend omissions or reductions convey negative information and are associated with future earnings problems.

A is incorrect because dividend initiations convey positive information and are associated with an expected increase (not a decrease) in future earnings growth. Dividend omissions or reductions convey negative information and are associated with future earnings problems.

B is incorrect because dividend initiations convey positive information and are associated with an expectation that future earnings growth will increase (not remain unchanged). In contrast, dividend omissions or reductions convey negative information and are associated with future earnings problems.

10. The appropriate matches are as follows:

Column A	Column B
1. Bird in the hand	a) Dividend policy matters
2. Homemade dividends	b) Dividend policy is irrelevant
3. High tax rates on dividends	a) Dividend policy matters

11. C is correct. The MM dividend theory assumes no taxes or transaction costs, but it does not assume investors have a preference for dividends over capital gains.

12. C is correct. Because the clientele for PAT investors has the same tax rate (zero) for dividends and capital gains, the ex-dividend stock price of PAT should decline by the amount of the dividend to €40 – €1.50 = €38.50. Chan will purchase €150,000/€38.50 = 3,896 additional shares. This increases her total shares owned to 103,896. Chan's new share ownership is closest to 103,900.

13. B is correct. A decrease in the quarterly dividend rate is likely to signal negative information. A decrease is typically understood as signaling poor future business prospects.

14. B is correct. The effective tax rate can be computed as 1 minus the fraction of 1 unit of earnings that investors retain after all taxes, or 1 – (1 – 0.40)(1 – 0.30) = 0.58 or 58% effective tax rate. Another way to obtain the solution: Corporate taxes = 1.00 × 0.40 = 0.40 and Personal taxes = 0.60 in dividends × 0.30 = 0.18, so Total tax = 0.40 + 0.18 = 0.58, or 58% effective rate.

15. C is correct. With low growth prospects, a company would typically have a high payout ratio, returning funds to its shareholders rather than retaining funds.

16. A is correct. The estimated dividend per share is US$0.68.

$$\text{Previous DPS} = \text{US\$0.60}$$

$$\text{Expected EPS} = \text{US\$4}$$

$$\text{Target payout ratio} = 0.25$$

$$\text{Five-year adjustment factor} = 1/5 = 0.2$$

Expected dividend = Previous dividend + (Expected earnings × Target payout ratio – Previous dividend) × Adjustment factor

$$= \text{US\$0.60} + [(\text{US\$4.00} \times 0.25 - \text{US\$0.60}) \times 0.2]$$
$$= \text{US\$0.60} + \text{US\$0.08}$$
$$= \text{US\$0.68}$$

17. B is correct. Choice A is consistent with a constant dividend target payout ratio policy. Choice C is not correct because the earnings increases described are not sustainable long term.

18. C is correct. At the current market price, the company can repurchase 200,000 shares (£10 million/£50 = 200,000 shares). The company would have 800,000 shares outstanding after the repurchase (1 million shares – 200,000 shares = 800,000 shares).

    EPS before the buyback is £2.00 (£2 million/1 million shares = £2.00). Total earnings after the buyback are the same because the company uses surplus (nonearning) cash to purchase the shares, but the number of shares outstanding is reduced to 800,000. EPS increases to £2.50 (£2 million/ 800,000 shares = £2.50).

19. B is correct. If the P/E is 32, the earnings-to-price ratio (earnings yield or E/P) is 1/32 = 3.125%. When the cost of capital is greater than the earnings yield, earnings dilution will result from the buyback.

20. A is correct. The company's earnings yield (E/P) is US$2/US$40 = 0.05. When the earnings yield is greater than the after-tax cost of borrowed funds, EPS will increase if shares are repurchased using borrowed funds.

21. A is correct.

> Total earnings before buyback: US$4.00 × 3,100,000 shares = US$12,400,000
> Total amount of borrowing: US$50 × 100,000 shares = US$5,000,000
> After-tax cost of borrowing the amount of funds needed: US$5,000,000 × 0.06 = US$300,000
> Number of shares outstanding after buyback: 3,100,000 - 100,000 = 3,000,000
> EPS after buyback: (US$12,400,000 - US$300,000)/3,000,000 shares = US$4.03

The P/E before the buyback is US$50/US$4 = 12.5; thus, the E/P is 8%. The after-tax cost of debt is 6%; therefore, EPS will increase.

22. C is correct. The company's book value before the buyback is €850 million in assets - €250 million in liabilities = €600 million. Book value per share is €600 million/20 million = €30 per share. The buyback will reduce equity by 2 million shares at the prevailing market price of €30 per share. The book value of equity will be reduced to €600 million - €60 million = €540 million, and the number of shares will be reduced to 18 million; €540 million/18 million = €30 book value per share. If the prevailing market price is equal to the book value per share at the time of the buyback, book value per share is unchanged.

23. C is correct. The prevailing market price is US$2.00(20) = US$40.00 per share; thus, the buyback would reduce equity by US$40 million. Book value of equity before the buyback is US$300 million. Book value of equity after the buyback would be US$300 million - US$40 million = US$260 million. The number of shares outstanding after the buyback would be 9 million. Thus, book value per share after the buyback would be US$260 million/9 million = US$28.89 ≈ US$29.

24. A is correct. Of the three methods, only an authorized open market share repurchase plan allows the company the flexibility to time share repurchases to coincide with share price declines.

25. C is correct. For the two options to be equivalent with respect to shareholders' wealth, the amount of cash distributed, the taxation, and the information content must be the same for both options.

26. C is correct. When there are no taxes, there are no tax differences between dividends and capital gains. All other things being equal, the effect on shareholder wealth of a dividend and a share repurchase should be the same.

27. A is correct. When capital gains are taxed at lower rates than dividends, investors may prefer companies that return cash to shareholders through share repurchases rather than dividends.

28. B is correct. Management sometimes undertakes share repurchases when it views shares as being undervalued in the marketplace.

29. C is correct. Shareholders would prefer that the company repurchase its shares instead of paying dividends when the tax rate on capital gains is lower than the tax rate on dividends.

CHAPTER 10

BUSINESS MODELS & RISKS

SOLUTIONS

1. C is correct. Financial forecasts are normally part of a more detailed business plan. A business model should convey how the business makes money, so unit economics (i.e., per-unit revenue and costs) are a key element of a business model. Based on the product and market, the target market (who the business serves), the channel strategy (where they purchase), and the total cost of ownership, including maintenance after purchase, would also be key business model elements.

2. C is correct. A business model that assumes premium pricing must address why customers will be willing to pay a premium, normally because of some type of differentiation. It is less likely (although not impossible) that a price premium could be sustained in a category where pricing is set in the market (A), where a small change in price causes a large change in demand (another way to describe the price taker scenario; D), or when a firm is trying to scale up to a competitive size (B).

3. E is correct. All these statements are true, in most cases, for a platform business. A platform business is defined as a business based on network effects—that is, where the value of its service or product is enhanced by the addition of customers or users. While many think of platform businesses as being web-based or software-based, there are many older business models that qualify, such as brokerage and exchange businesses and transportation and communication networks. The value creation for a platform business is external to the company that created the product or service. When the business is launched, it has no customers, which can make the launch challenging—one reason why many platform startups employ a "freemium" pricing strategy to attract users quickly.

4. E is correct. The resume preparation service benefits from the network effects on various online job sites, but the service is not the source of those network effects. Each of the other businesses (A, B, C, and D) becomes more valuable to its customers as it attracts users. A stock exchange is valuable and worth joining because many securities trade on it. The telephone network is very useful because most people are on it. A classified advertising website becomes more useful as it attracts more listings. An airfare price comparison website is valuable to airlines because it has many shoppers and valuable to shoppers because it features prices for multiple airlines and routes.

5. C is correct. A supply chain includes all the steps involved in producing and delivering a physical product to the end customer, regardless of whether those steps are performed by a single firm. A value chain includes only those functions performed by a single firm, but it also includes functions that are valuable to customers but may not involve physical transformation or handling of the product. The bicycle delivery service is a source of

value to customers, so it is part of the flower shop's value proposition, but it is performed by a third party, so it is not part of the flower shop value chain but, rather, is part of its supply chain. The answering service is not a step in the physical goods flow, so it is not a part of the supply chain.

6. C is correct. A social network for model train collectors involves a single group of users and thus is closest to a one-sided network. The others involve two user groups: employers and job-seekers in A, men and women in B, and homeowners and contractors in D.

7. A is correct. Unit costs normally include direct labor costs. A unit cost analysis should be considered in most business models, although in some cases, they will be close to zero (for example, digital media). If unit costs are non-zero, they must be taken into account when calculating the break-even point. In D, there are no direct labor costs, so the unit cost calculation is reasonable. (The lemonade stand is staffed, and no extra labor is required to pour the lemonade.)

8. B is correct. Macro risk is likely to be highest with a Swedish mining equipment manufacturer since product demand is very sensitive to the global economy. With the coffee plantation in Brazil, the call center outsourcing business based in India, and the Swedish mining equipment manufacturer, there is also exchange rate risk that could impact profitability and competitiveness.

9. C is correct. An oil well drilling service company operates in a highly competitive industry, where demand is difficult to forecast and is very sensitive to macro risk. Industry risk is therefore likely to be high. The toll road and the pest control services company have recurring, predictable revenues with significant "moats" or barriers to competition.

10. Option 1 (Demand falls gradually due to a declining population) matches with B (Macro risk). That demand falls gradually due to a declining population is a macro risk because it impacts all business and economic activities.

    Option 2 (Consumer tastes shift to favor locally manufactured apparel) matches with C (Industry risk). That consumer tastes shift to favor locally manufactured apparel is an industry risk that impacts all apparel manufacturing businesses in similar fashion.

    Option 3 (The company faces uncertainty about future demand as it hires a new chief designer and makes changes to its top-selling products) matches with A (Company-specific risk). That the company faces uncertainty about future demand as it hires a new chief designer and makes changes to its top-selling products is a company-specific risk because it is within the company management's direct control and does not impact other businesses.

11. C is correct. A company with consistent operating margins and a stable market share in a highly specialized business embarks on a significant and ambitious strategic change. Its success will depend entirely on how well management succeeds in delivering on its objective by improving margins (either by increasing prices or reducing costs) and taking market share from its competitors. Considering the relatively small size of the business, it may be difficult. Considering that many manufacturing businesses in the same industry typically operate around similar margins, any margin improvement may be difficult. That a manufacturer replaces aging factory machinery with similar but more efficient equipment is not an example of execution risk; it is part of regular improvement and capital investment. That a marketer of high-fashion pet accessories tests the market to see if there is demand for glamourous dog harnesses made with faux fur is a standard and common expansion of an existing product line with limited risk.

12. A is correct. Reducing prices decreases the business's margin, and as such, it increases its sensitivity to changes in demand, revenue, and costs and its operating leverage. The choice between debt and equity financing has no bearing on operating leverage, although it should be noted that interest expenses on debt are contractually determined payments, while dividends are discretionary payments. Using casual labor rather than a salaried work force reduces the fixed employee expenses, which reduces operating leverage.

13. C is correct. Entering a sale–leaseback transaction for the company's head office building increases financial leverage. The company sells assets with the obligation to repurchase the assets in the future as well as make lease payments. These transactions increase its financial leverage. Additionally, sale and leaseback transactions reduce the business's overall asset base, which, in turn, reduces its ability to add more debt should the company need to raise debt. Cutting prices reduces the profit margin for the business, thereby increasing operating leverage. Replacing short-term debt with long-term debt does not change financial leverage: Debt, irrespective of maturity, is simply debt.

CHAPTER 11

THE FIRM AND MARKET STRUCTURES

SOLUTIONS

1. C is correct. Monopolistic competition is characterized by many sellers, differentiated products, and some pricing power.
2. A is correct. Few sellers of a homogeneous or standardized product characterizes an oligopoly.
3. B is correct. The long-run competitive equilibrium occurs where MC = AC = P for each company. Equating MC and AC implies $2 + 8Q = 256/Q + 2 + 4Q$.

    Solving for Q gives $Q = 8$. Equating MC with price gives $P = 2 + 8Q = 66$. Any price above 66 yields an economic profit because $P = $ MC > AC, so new companies will enter the market.
4. B is correct. The economic profit will attract new entrants to the market and encourage existing companies to expand capacity.
5. C is correct. The profit maximizing choice is the level of output where marginal revenue equals marginal cost.
6. A is correct. The oligopolist faces two different demand structures, one for price increases and another for price decreases. Competitors will lower prices to match a price reduction, but will not match a price increase. The result is a kinked demand curve.
7. B is correct. When companies have similar market shares, competitive forces tend to outweigh the benefits of collusion.
8. B is correct. The credible threat of entry holds down prices and multiple incumbents are offering undifferentiated products.
9. C is correct. There are many competitors in the market, but some product differentiation exists, as the price differential between Deep River's brand and the house brands indicates.
10. C is correct. In the Nash model, each company considers the other's reaction in selecting its strategy. In equilibrium, neither company has an incentive to change its strategy. ThetaTech is better off with open architecture regardless of what SigmaSoft decides. Given this choice, SigmaSoft is better off with a proprietary platform. Neither company will change its decision unilaterally.
11. B is correct. A company in a perfectly competitive market must accept whatever price the market dictates. The marginal cost schedule of a company in a perfectly competitive market determines its supply function.

12. A is correct. As prices decrease, smaller companies will leave the market rather than sell below cost. The market share of Aquarius, the price leader, will increase.

13. B is correct. The dominant company's market share tends to decrease as profits attract entry by other companies.

14. B is correct. The product produced in a perfectly competitive market cannot be differentiated by advertising or any other means.

15. C is correct. Profits are maximized when MR = MC. For a monopoly, MR = $P[1 - 1/E_p]$. Setting this equal to MC and solving for P:

$40 = P[1 - (1/1.5)] = P \times 0.333$

$P = 120

16. B is correct. This allows the investors to receive a normal return for the risk they are taking in the market.

17. B is correct. The top four companies in the industry comprise 86 percent of industry sales: (300 + 250 + 200 + 150)/(300 + 250 + 200 + 150 + 100 + 50) = 900/1050 = 86%.

18. B is correct. The three-firm Herfindahl–Hirschmann Index is $0.35^2 + 0.25^2 + 0.20^2 = 0.225$.

19. B is correct. The Herfindahl–Hirschmann Index does not reflect low barriers to entry that may restrict the market power of companies currently in the market.

CHAPTER 12

INTRODUCTION TO INDUSTRY AND COMPANY ANALYSIS

SOLUTIONS

1. C is correct. Tactical asset allocation involves timing investments in asset classes and does not make use of industry analysis.
2. C is correct. A sector rotation strategy is conducted by investors wishing to time investment in industries through an analysis of fundamentals and/or business-cycle conditions.
3. B is correct. Determination of a company's competitive environment depends on understanding its industry.
4. B is correct. Business-cycle sensitivity falls on a continuum and is not a discrete "either/ or" phenomenon.
5. C is correct. Cyclical companies are sensitive to the business cycle, with low product demand during periods of economic contraction and high product demand during periods of economic expansion. They, therefore, experience wider-than-average fluctuations in product demand.
6. C is correct. Customers' flexibility as to when they purchase a product makes the product more sensitive to the business cycle.
7. C is correct. Varying conditions of recession or expansion around the world would affect the comparisons of companies with sales in different regions of the world.
8. B is correct. Personal care products are classified as consumer staples in the "Description of Representative Sectors."
9. C is correct. Automobile manufacturers are classified as consumer discretionary. Consumer discretionary companies derive a majority of revenue from the sale of consumer-related products for which demand tends to exhibit a high degree of economic sensitivity—that is, high demand during periods of economic expansion and low demand during periods of contraction.
10. C is correct. Commercial systems are generally updated more frequently than government systems and include only publicly traded for-profit companies.
11. B is correct. Constructing a peer group is a subjective process, and a logical starting point is to begin with a commercially available classification system. This system will identify a

group of companies that may have properties comparable to the business activity of interest.

12. A is correct because it is a false statement. Reviewing the annual report to find management's discussion about the competitive environment and specific competitors is a suggested step in the process of constructing a peer group.

13. B is correct. The company could be in more than one peer group depending on the demand drivers for the business segments, although the multiple business segments may make it difficult to classify the company.

14. C is correct. For the automobile industry, the high capital requirements and other elements mentioned in the reading provide high barriers to entry, and recognition that auto factories are generally only of use for manufacturing cars implies a high barrier to exit.

15. C is correct. A slow pace of product innovation often means that customers prefer to stay with suppliers they know, implying stable market shares.

16. C is correct. Capacity increases in providing insurance services would not involve several factors that would be important to the other two industries, including the need for substantial fixed capital investments or, in the case of a restaurant, outfitting rental or purchased space. These requirements would tend to slow down, respectively, steel production and restaurant expansion.

17. C is correct. The embryonic stage is characterized by slow growth and high prices.

18. C is correct. The growth phase is not likely to experience price wars because expanding industry demand provides companies the opportunity to grow even without increasing market share. When industry growth is stagnant, companies may only be able to grow by increasing market share—for example, by engaging in price competition.

19. B is correct. The industry life-cycle model shows how demand evolves over time as an industry passes from the embryonic stage through the stage of decline.

20. A is correct. Industry consolidation and relatively high barriers to entry are two characteristics of a mature-stage industry.

21. C is correct. The relatively few members of the industry generally try to avoid price competition.

22. C is correct. With short lead times, industry capacity can be rapidly increased to satisfy demand, but it may also lead to overcapacity and lower profits.

23. A is correct. An industry that has high barriers to entry generally requires substantial physical capital and/or financial investment. With weak pricing power in the industry, finding a buyer for excess capacity (i.e., to exit the industry) may be difficult.

24. C is correct. Economic profit is earned and value is created for shareholders when the industry earns returns above the company's cost of capital.

25. B is correct. The alcoholic beverage industry is concentrated and possesses strong pricing power.

26. B is correct. Vision typically deteriorates at advanced ages. An increased number of older adults implies more eyewear products will be purchased.

27. B is correct. As their educational level increases, workers are able to perform more skilled tasks, earn higher wages, and as a result, have more income left for discretionary expenditures.

28. A is correct. Seeking economies of scale would tend to reduce per-unit costs and increase profit.

29. A is correct. Companies with low-cost strategies must be able to invest in productivity-improving equipment and finance that investment at a low cost of capital. Market share and pricing depend on whether the strategy is pursued defensively or offensively.

30. A is correct. The cost structure is an appropriate element when analyzing the supply of the product, but analysis of demand relies on the product's differentiating characteristics and the customers' needs and wants.

31. C is correct. The corporate profile would provide an understanding of these elements.

CHAPTER 13

FINANCIAL STATEMENT MODELING

SOLUTIONS

1. C is correct. Economies of scale are a situation in which average costs decrease with increasing sales volume. Chrome's gross margins have been increasing with net sales. Gross margins that increase with sales levels provide evidence of economies of scale, assuming that higher levels of sales reflect increased unit sales. Gross margin more directly reflects the cost of sales than does profit margin.

Metric	2017	2018	2019
Net sales	$46.8	$50.5	$53.9
Gross profit	28.6	32.1	35.1
Gross margin (gross profit/net sales)	61.11%	63.56%	65.12%

2. A is correct. A bottom-up approach for developing inputs to equity valuation models begins at the level of the individual company or a unit within the company. By modeling net sales using the average annual growth rate, Candidate A is using a bottom-up approach. Both Candidate B and Candidate C are using a top-down approach, which begins at the level of the overall economy.

3. B is correct. A top-down approach usually begins at the level of the overall economy. Candidate B assumes industry sales will grow at the same rate as nominal GDP but that Chrome will have a 2 percentage point decline in market share. Candidate B is not using any elements of a bottom-up approach; therefore, a hybrid approach is not being employed.

4. C is correct. Candidate C assumes that the 2020 gross margin will increase by 20 bps from 2019 and that net sales will grow at 50 bps slower than nominal GDP (nominal GDP = Real GDP + Inflation = 1.6% + 2.0% = 3.6%). Accordingly, the 2020 forecasted cost of sales is USD19.27 million, rounded to USD19.3 million.

Metric	Calculation	Result
2020 gross margin = 2019 gm + 20 bps	$35.1/$53.9 = 65.12% + 0.20% = 65.32%	
2020 CoS/net sales = 100% – gross margin	100% – 65.32% =	34.68%
2020 net sales = 2019 net sales × (1 + Nominal GDP – 0.50%)	$53.9 million × (1 + 0.036 – 0.005) = $53.9 million × 1.031 =	$55.57 million
2020 cost of sales = 2020 net sales × CoS/net sales	$55.57 × 34.68% =	$19.27 million

5. B is correct. Candidate A assumes that the 2020 SG&A/net sales will be the same as the average SG&A/net sales over the 2017–19 time period and that net sales will grow at the annual average growth rate in net sales over the 2017–19 time period. Accordingly, the 2020 forecasted SG&A expenses are USD25.5 million.

Metric	Calculation	Result
Average SG&A/net sales, 2017–2019*	(41.24% + 44.55% + 46.57%)/3 =	44.12%
Average annual growth sales in net sales, 2017–2019**	(7.91% + 6.73%)/2 =	7.32%
2020 net sales = 2019 net sales × (1 + Average annual growth rate in net sales)	$53.9 million × 1.0732 =	$57.85 million
2020 SG&A = 2020 net sales × Average SG&A/net sales	$57.85 million × 44.12% =	$25.52 million

* SG&A/net sales are calculated as follows:

	2017	2018	2019
Net Sales	$46.8	$50.5	$53.9
SG&A expenses	$19.3	$22.5	$25.1
SG&A-to-sales ratio	41.24%	44.55%	46.57%

** Growth rate in net sales is calculated as follows:

Year	Calculation
2018	($50.5/$46.8) – 1 = 7.91%
2019	($53.9/$50.5) – 1 = 6.73%

6. A is correct. In forecasting financing costs, such as interest expense, the debt/equity structure of a company is a key determinant. Accordingly, a method that recognizes the relationship between the income statement account (interest expense) and the balance sheet account (debt) would be a preferable method for forecasting interest expense when compared with methods that forecast based solely on the income statement account. By using the effective interest rate (interest expense divided by average gross debt), Candidate A is taking the debt/equity structure into account. Candidate B (who forecasts 2020 interest expense to be the same as 2019 interest expense) and Candidate C (who forecasts 2020 interest expense to be the same as the 2017–19 average interest expense) are not taking the balance sheet into consideration.

7. B is correct. Base rates refer to attributes of a reference class and base rate neglect is ignoring such class information in favor of specific information. By incorporating industry data, Candidate B is seeking to mitigate this.

8. B is correct. Operating (EBIT) margin is a pre-tax profitability measure that can be useful in the peer comparison of companies in countries with different tax structures. Archway's two main competitors are located in different countries with significantly different tax structures; therefore, a pre-tax measure is better than an after-tax measure, such as ROIC. The current ratio is a liquidity measure, not a profitability measure.

9. A is correct. Porter's five forces framework in Exhibit 1 describes an industry with high barriers to entry, high customer switching costs (suggesting a low threat of substitutes), and a specialized product (suggesting low bargaining power of buyers). Furthermore, the primary production inputs from the large group of suppliers are considered basic commodities (suggesting low bargaining power of suppliers). These favorable industry characteristics will likely enable Archway to pass along price increases and generate above-average returns on invested capital.

10. A is correct. The current favorable characteristics of the industry (high barriers to entry, low bargaining power of suppliers and buyers, low threat of substitutes), coupled with Archway's dominant market share position, will likely lead to Archway's profit margins being at least equal to or greater than current levels over the forecast horizon.

11. C is correct. The calculation of Archway's gross profit margin for 2020, which reflects the industry-wide 8% inflation on COGS, is calculated as follows:

Revenue growth	1.85%
COGS increase	4.76%
Forecasted revenue (Base revenue = 100)	101.85
Forecasted COGS (Base COGS = 30)	31.43
Forecasted gross profit	70.42
Forecasted gross profit margin	69.14%

$$\text{Revenue growth} = (1 + \text{Price increase for revenue}) \times (1 + \text{Volume growth}) - 1$$
$$= (1.05) \times (0.97) - 1$$
$$= 1.85\%.$$

$$\text{COGS increase} = (1 + \text{Price increase for COGS}) \times (1 + \text{Volume growth}) - 1$$
$$= (1.08) \times (0.97) - 1$$
$$= 4.76\%.$$

$$\text{Forecasted revenue} = \text{Base revenue} \times \text{Revenue growth increase}$$
$$= 100 \times 1.0185$$
$$= 101.85.$$

$$\text{Forecasted COGS} = \text{Base COGS} \times \text{COGS increase}$$
$$= 30 \times 1.0476$$
$$= 31.43.$$

$$\text{Forecasted gross profit} = \text{Forecasted revenue} - \text{Forecasted COGS}$$
$$= 101.85 - 31.43$$
$$= 70.42.$$

$$\text{Forecasted gross profit margin} = \text{Forecasted gross profit/Forecasted revenue}$$
$$= 70.42/101.85$$
$$= 69.14\%.$$

12. C is correct. French is using a bottom-up approach to forecast Archway's working capital accounts by using the company's historical efficiency ratios to project future performance.
13. B is correct. If the future growth or profitability of a company is likely to be lower than the historical average (in this case, because of a potential technological development), then the target multiple should reflect a discount to the historical multiple to reflect this difference in growth and/or profitability. If a multiple is used to derive the terminal value of a company, the choice of the multiple should be consistent with the long-run expectations for growth and required return. French tells Wright he believes that such a technological development could have an adverse impact on Archway beyond the forecast horizon.
14. C is correct. Forecasting a single scenario would not be appropriate given the high degree of uncertainty and range of potential outcomes for companies in this industry.
15. B is correct. Small, inexpensive, imported petrol-fueled motorcycles are substitutes for petrol scooters and could increasingly have an impact on Omikroon's petrol scooter pricing power.
16. B is correct. Return on invested capital is net operating profit minus adjusted taxes divided by invested capital, where invested capital is defined as operating assets minus operating liabilities.
17. A is correct. Competition from other electric scooter manufacturers is expected to begin in one year. After this time, competing electric scooters could lead to lower demand for Omikroon's electric scooters and affect Omikroon's gross profit margin.
18. B is correct. The electric scooter market is expected to grow rapidly, so the contribution of Omrikoon's new electric scooter division is forecast to expand significantly over the

next 10 years. A is not correct because the investment company's portfolio turnover is not relevant for forecasting Omnrikoon's future results. C is not correct because the light truck division is expected to add only 2% to total revenues in the future.

19. A is correct. The sensitivity analysis consists of an increase of 20% in the price of an input that constitutes 4% of cost of sales. Change in gross profit margin because of that increase is calculated as the change in cost of sales because of price increase divided by sales:

$$= (\text{Cost of sales} \times 0.04 \times 0.2)/\text{Sales}$$
$$= (105.38 \times 0.04 \times 0.2)/152.38$$
$$= 0.0055$$

20. C is correct. In Scenario 2, growth capital expenditure of EUR27 million for the refit of the existing idle factory is higher than the growth capital expenditure in Scenario 1 of EUR25 million. The EUR25 million is the cost of building a new factory for EUR30 million less the proceeds from the sale of the existing idle factory of EUR5 million.

21. C is correct. The management of Omikroom and investor relations of ZeroWheel are almost certainly biased in favor of expecting strong growth for the markets they participate in. To evaluate the forecast, Fromm should seek more independent sources and balance the biased sources with sources biased in the opposite direction or an analyst who is more skeptical.

CHAPTER 14

CORPORATE RESTRUCTURINGS

SOLUTIONS

1. C is correct. Jupiter is undertaking a sale-leaseback transaction, which is a type of balance sheet restructuring. Jupiter would receive cash from the property sales and recognize a liability equal to the present value of future lease payments. A is incorrect because a reorganization is a court-supervised restructuring process available in most jurisdictions for companies facing insolvency from burdensome debt levels and, sometimes, as a strategic measure to renegotiate contracts with unfavorable terms. B is incorrect because a cost restructuring refers to actions whose goal is to reduce costs by improving operational efficiency and profitability, often to bring margins to a historical level or to those of comparable industry peers.

2. C is correct. The sale leasebacks will improve Jupiter's balance sheet by retiring debt and likely improving its credit rating, which will decrease (not increase) its costs of capital. A is incorrect because real estate ownership represents a non-core business for Jupiter. Its core business is operating 50,000 square foot stores in all markets of the United States. B is incorrect because the sale leasebacks will allow Jupiter to unlock the value in its real estate assets. Jupiter would receive cash from the property sales and recognize a liability equal to the present value of future lease payments.

3. A is correct. Jupiter's average capitalization rate for the sale-leaseback transactions is 5.50%, which is supported by the median of the 25th, 50th, and 75th percentile cap rates for sale transactions for similarly situated properties with similar lease terms in the last three years (5.00%, 5.50%, and 6.00%). B and C are incorrect because Jupiter's average capitalization rate for the sale-leaseback transactions is 5.50%, which is supported by the median of the 25th, 50th, and 75th percentile cap rates for sale transactions for similarly situated properties with similar lease terms in the last three years (5.00%, 5.50%, and 6.00%).

4. C is correct. USD421,440 million is calculated as follows:

$$\text{Upstream: USD14,400} \times 19 = \text{USD273,600.}$$

$$\text{Midstream: USD5,760} \times 17 = \text{USD97,920.}$$

$$\text{Downstream: USD3,840} \times 13 = \text{USD49,920.}$$

$$\text{Consolidated: USD421,440 million}$$

A is incorrect because USD392,000 million is incorrectly calculated by using the average of the peer segment multiples $[(19 + 17 + 13)/3 = 16.33]$ to estimate the consolidated enterprise value.

$$\text{Upstream: USD14,400} \times 16.33 = \text{USD234,720.}$$

$$\text{Midstream: USD5,760} \times 16.33 = \text{USD93.888.}$$

$$\text{Downstream: USD3,840} \times 16.33 = \text{USD62,592.}$$

$$\text{Consolidated: USD392,000 million}$$

B is incorrect because USD408,000 million is Saturn's current enterprise value, not the estimated enterprise value based on median peer multiples for all three segments.

5. B is correct. An advantage of the comparable company analysis method is that estimates of value are derived directly from the market. This approach is unlike the discounted cash flow method, in which the value is determined based on many assumptions and estimates. A is incorrect because the comparable company analysis method is sensitive to market mispricing. As an example, suppose that all the comparable companies are currently overvalued by the market. A valuation relative to those companies may suggest a value that is too high in the sense that values would be revised downward upon a correction. C is incorrect because the comparable company analysis method provides a reasonable approximation of a target company's value relative to similar companies (not transactions) in the market. It assumes that "like" assets should be valued on a similar basis in the market.

6. B is correct. The forecasted operating income in Year 3 is calculated as follows:

Combined Stratton and Midwest Oil: Year 1–3 Figures (USD millions)

	Year 1	Year 2	Year 3
Revenues			
Stratton	21,325	22,391	23,511
Add: Midwest revenues	5,350	5,618	5,898
Combined revenues	**26,675**	**28,009**	**29,409**
Operating expenses			
Stratton	16,525	17,351	18,219
Add: Midwest	3,050	3,203	3,363
Subtract: synergies	(117)	(233)	(350)
Add: one-time costs	175	280	395
Combined operating expenses	**19,633**	**20,601**	**21,627**
Operating income (Rev-OpEx)	**7,042**	**7,408**	**7,782**

A is incorrect because it incorrectly excludes Year 3 synergies of USD350 million. C is incorrect because it incorrectly excludes Year 3 one-time costs of USD395 million.

7. C is correct. Materiality can be defined along two dimensions: size and fit. Although the acquisition does not signal a change in strategy or focus for Stratton, the transaction is considered large and material because it exceeds 10% of Stratton's enterprise value prior to the transaction. The total consideration is USD90 billion, based on share prices just prior to the announcement; thus, it represents 13.8% of Stratton's enterprise value just prior to the announcement of USD650 billion. A is incorrect because materiality can be defined along two dimensions: size and fit. Although the acquisition does not signal a change in strategy or focus for Stratton, the transaction is considered large and material because it exceeds 10% of Stratton's enterprise value prior to the transaction. B is incorrect because the transaction is considered large and material because it exceeds 10% of Stratton's enterprise value prior to the transaction.

8. B is correct. Following the close of the acquisition, Stratton expects its outstanding debt to total USD62 billion, after assuming USD4.3 billion in existing Midwest debt and issuing USD26 billion. Therefore, prior to the acquisition, Stratton had approximately (62 − 4.3 − 26 =) USD31.7 billion in debt and (1.096 billion shares outstanding × USD125 per share =) USD137.0 billion in equity, resulting in a mix of debt and equity of 19% and 81%, respectively. After the acquisition, Stratton will have USD62 billion in debt and (1.096 billion + 104 million =) 1.2 billion shares outstanding, which, priced at USD125 per share, results in USD150 billion in equity, resulting in a mix of debt and equity of 29% and 71%, respectively. The change in capital structure is summarized below.

Stratton's Capital Structure before and after Acquisition of Midwest

Stratton Capital Structure	Pre-Acquisition	Post-Acquisition
Debt %	19%	29%
Equity %	81%	71%

A is incorrect because 29% represents the percentage of debt after acquisition. C is incorrect because 81% represents the percentage of equity prior to acquisition.

9. A is correct. Acquisitions require substantially greater capital investments than equity investments. Acquisitions—not equity investments—allow the acquirer to gain control of the target. Relative to equity investments, joint ventures provide more equal governance representation and require larger investments. B is incorrect because acquisitions (not equity investments) allow the acquirer to gain control of the target. C is incorrect because relative to equity investments, joint ventures provide more equal governance representation and require larger investments.

10. C is correct. The estimated conglomerate discount just prior to the announcement is calculated as follows: Total estimated enterprise value from sum-of-the-parts valuation − Current trading enterprise value = USD187 billion − USD170 billion = USD17 billion. A is incorrect because it incorrectly subtracts the estimated enterprise value from the current trading enterprise value. B is incorrect because the estimated and current trading enterprise values are not equal.

CHAPTER 15

ENVIRONMENTAL, SOCIAL, AND GOVERNANCE (ESG) CONSIDERATIONS IN INVESTMENT ANALYSIS

SOLUTIONS

1. C is correct. Yorkton uses the proprietary method to identify company and industry ESG factors. This approach relies on using company-specific ESG data that is publicly available from annual reports, proxy reports, corporate sustainability reports, and regulatory filings such as the 10-K. The problem is inconsistent reporting of ESG information and metrics among firms. The level of disclosure also varies considerably among companies because ESG-related disclosures are voluntary. This creates comparability issues for analysts.

   A is incorrect because the promotion of uniform accounting standards is an alternative approach used to identify ESG reports. This approach involves not-for-profit initiatives and sustainability reporting frameworks that develop a standardized framework of ESG disclosures in corporate reporting. As an example, the Sustainable Accounting Standards Board (SASB) seeks to promote uniform accounting standards.

   B is incorrect because it relates to an alternative approach to identifying company and industry ESG factors. This approach involves using information supplied by ESG data vendors, such MSCI or Sustainalytics. The vendors provide ESG scores and/or rankings for each company. The problem with this approach is the subjective element to the interpretation of ESG scores and rankings.

2. C is correct. In identifying a company's ESG risks and opportunities, an analyst must determine which ESG factors are relevant to its industry. Industries such as energy and steel are typically more impacted by environmental factors. This is clearly the case with Titian. Titian's steel production is energy intensive and relies on coal in producing its main product, stainless steel. Its major customers are oil and natural gas companies, and most of its steel capacity is located in developing economies, where it currently faces few environmental regulations. Changes in such regulations and projected declining demand for its main product are major risk factors for the firm.

   A is incorrect because social factors are typically not the most important industry-related ESG risk factors for steel companies. Employee health and safety is a material social factor for this company. This is not a risk since the company has an excellent record on employee health and safety.

B is incorrect because governance factors are not a major risk for Titian. Titian's board comprises 10 members, of whom 5 are independent. In addition, the board has gender diversity and no CEO duality, since the chairperson is not the CEO.

3. B is correct. Statement 2 is correct because the level of disclosure varies considerably among companies since ESG-related disclosures are voluntary. This creates a comparability issue for analysts. This is a problem associated with the proprietary methods used to identify company and industry ESG factors.

    A is incorrect because Statement 1 is incorrect. The problems in doing ESG investment analysis based on company information are that the reporting of this information is inconsistent and that disclosures vary among companies.

    C is incorrect because Statement 3 is incorrect. The time horizon is an important factor affecting the materiality of the underlying ESG factors. Some ESG issues may affect a company's performance in the short term, whereas other issues may be more relevant in the long term. This is especially true in credit analysis because of the different maturities of the bonds.

4. Titian faces long-term risk from *stranded assets* due to potential regulatory changes in the developing economies.

    If regulatory changes on greenhouse gas emissions are enacted in these developing economies, much of Titian's stainless steel capacity will become obsolete or not economically viable. This will result in ESG-related adjustments to Titian's balance sheet. The further reduction in oil demand will make the steel capacity economically unviable.

5. B is correct. Titian faces significant long-term environmental risk factors. The imposition of stricter regulation on greenhouse gas emissions in the developing countries will result in stranded assets, as much of Titian steel capacity becomes obsolete and not economically viable. Shifting away from low-cost coal usage will likely result in higher operating costs, and declining oil and natural gas demand will result in lower revenues for stainless steel. Thus Yorkton should raise the discount rate for Titian to account for the higher environmental risk.

    A is incorrect because Titian's revenues are likely to decline as a result of the projected fall in demand for oil and natural gas. As a result, oil and natural gas companies will cut their exploration and drilling budgets and reduce their purchases of stainless steel.

    C is incorrect since operating costs are likely to rise as Titian shifts away from using low-cost coal to more expensive energy sources.

6. A is correct. The stock price for Titian is likely to decline. Titian faces significant long-term environmental risk as a result of more stringent future regulation on greenhouse gas emissions in the developing economies and a future decline in demand for its main product, stainless steel. Thus in the discount cash flow model, Titian should increase the cost of equity and most likely lower the growth rate in cash flow. Both factors will cause the price to fall.

    B is incorrect since the price of Titian is likely to decline and not remain unchanged.

    C is incorrect since the price of Titian is likely to decline and not increase.

7. C is correct. BR Hotels has concentrated ownership, given that the family owns 55% of the shares. It also has concentrated voting power, since each ownership share has equal

voting rights. In this ownership structure, the controlling shareholders have power over both management and minority shareholders. The controlling shareholders are referred to as strong shareholders and the managers as weak managers. The conflict in this structure exists between the controlling shareholders and the minority shareholders. The controlling shareholders can potentially divert resources for their own benefit at the expense of the minority shareholders. This conflict is referred to as a principal-principal problem.

A is incorrect since the conflict for BR Hotels is a principal-principal problem. Voting caps are legal restrictions on the voting rights of large share positions. They result from an ownership structure of concentrated ownership and dispersed voting rights.

B is incorrect since the conflict for BR Hotels is a principal-principal problem. The principal-agent problem occurs when the ownership structure has dispersed ownership and dispersed voting rights. In this case, the structure has weak shareholders and strong management, with a potentially significant conflict between the shareholders and the management.

8. C is correct. The corporate governance risk for BR Hotels is high due to a low percentage of independent board members. Of the 15 members on the board, only one is independent. Many OECD countries have introduced a recommendation for the minimum ratio of independent directors serving on the board. They typically set the minimum ratio of independent directors in a range of 20%–50% or greater. BR Hotels falls below this range.

A is incorrect since CEO duality is not a governance problem for BR Hotels. BR Hotels' CEO and chairperson are separate, so there is no CEO duality. This is typically a sign of effective corporate governance. The independent chairperson and CEO roles help protect investor interests.

B is incorrect because family control is not likely to increase governance risk for BR Hotels. Family control lowers the risks associated with principal-agent problems. This is the result of the family's having concentrated ownership and management responsibility. The lower risk associated with the principal-agent problem is somewhat offset by the drawbacks of family control, which include poor transparency, modest considerations for minority shareholder rights, and difficulty in attracting quality management talent.

9. A is correct. The implementation of ESG factors in security analysis differs for equity analysis and fixed-income analysis. For BK Hotels' corporate bonds, the focus of ESG integration is on mitigating downside risk. In contrast, in equity analysis, ESG integration is used to both identify potential opportunities and mitigate downside risk.

B is incorrect since adjusting the discount rate is typically used in equity analysis and not in fixed-income analysis. In valuing a stock, an analyst may choose to adjust the discount factor to account for the ESG risk. In fixed-income analysis, the credit spread or CDS is adjusted to reflect the ESG risk.

C is incorrect since identifying potential opportunities is used in equity analysis and not in fixed-income analysis. In fixed-income analysis, the focus of ESG integration is on mitigating downside risk. In equity analysis, ESG integration is used to both identify potential opportunities and mitigate downside risk.

10. C is correct. BR Hotels faces significant corporate governance and social risk. Corporate governance risk is high due to a low number of independent board members (1 out of 15 members), lack of gender diversity (2 women out of 15 members), and low percentage of board members with hotel industry experience (20%). These factors are likely to increase

investors' perception of the corporation's risk. The social risk for BR Hotels is also high. BR Hotels has a high labor turnover rate, pays most of its workforce at or near the minimum wage, and offers no health benefits. Legislation raising the minimum wage and the growing pressure on BR Hotels to offer benefits would increase operating costs. This could have a negative impact on future cash flows, which would be detrimental to the bond holders. The valuation of BR Hotels' bonds could be adversely affected by the higher ESG risk. To account for the higher ESG risk, the credit spread on BR Hotels' bonds is likely to increase.

A is incorrect since the credit spread on BR Hotels' bonds is likely to increase and not decrease.

B is incorrect since the credit spread on BR Hotels' bonds is likely to increase and not remain unchanged.

CHAPTER 16

INTERCORPORATE INVESTMENTS

SOLUTIONS

1. B is correct. Under IFRS 9, FVPL and FVOCI securities are carried at market value, whereas amortized cost securities are carried at historical cost. €28,000 + 37,000 + 50,000 = €115,000.

2. C is correct. If Dumas had been classified as a FVPL security, its carrying value would have been the €55,000 fair value rather than the €50,000 historical cost.

3. B is correct. The coupon payment is recorded as interest income whether securities are amortized cost or FVPL. No adjustment is required for amortization since the bonds were bought at par.

4. C is correct. Unrealized gains and losses are included in income when securities are classified as FVPL. During 2018 there was an unrealized gain of €1,000.

5. B is correct. The difference between historical cost and par value must be amortized under the effective interest method. If the par value is less than the initial cost (stated interest rate is greater than the effective rate), the interest income would be lower than the interest received because of amortization of the premium.

6. B is correct. Under IFRS, SPEs must be consolidated if they are conducted for the benefit of the sponsoring entity. Further, under IFRS, SPEs cannot be classified as qualifying. Under US GAAP, qualifying SPEs (a classification that has been eliminated) do not have to be consolidated.

7. B is correct. If Cinnamon is deemed to have control over Cambridge, it would use the acquisition method to account for Cambridge and prepare consolidated financial statements. Proportionate consolidation is used for joint ventures; the equity method is used for some joint ventures and when there is significant influence but not control.

8. A is correct. If Cinnamon is deemed to have control over Cambridge, consolidated financial statements would be prepared and Cinnamon's total shareholders' equity would increase and include the amount of the noncontrolling interest. If Cinnamon is deemed to have significant influence, the equity method would be used and there would be no change in the total shareholders' equity of Cinnamon.

9. C is correct. If Cinnamon is deemed to have significant influence, it would report half of Cambridge's net income as a line item on its income statement, but no additional revenue is shown. Its profit margin is thus higher than if it consolidated Cambridge's

results, which would impact revenue and income, or if it only reported 19 percent of Cambridge's dividends (no change in ownership).

10. C is correct. The full and partial goodwill method will have the same amount of debt; however, shareholders' equity will be higher under full goodwill (and the debt to equity ratio will be lower). Therefore, the debt to equity will be higher under partial goodwill. If control is assumed, Cinnamon cannot use the equity method.

11. A is correct. Cambridge has a lower operating margin (88/1,100 = 8.0%) than Cinnamon (142/1,575 = 9.0%). If Cambridge's results are consolidated with Cinnamon's, the consolidated operating margin will reflect that of the combined company, or 230/2,675 = 8.6%.

12. A is correct. When a company is deemed to have control of another entity, it records all of the other entity's assets on its own consolidated balance sheet.

13. B is correct. If Zimt is deemed to have significant influence, it would use the equity method to record its ownership. Under the equity method, Zimt's share of Oxbow's net income would be recorded as a single line item. Net income of Zimt = 75 + 0.5(68) = 109.

14. B is correct. Under the proportionate consolidation method, Zimt's balance sheet would show its own total liabilities of €1,421 – 735 = €686 plus half of Oxbow's liabilities of €1,283 – 706 = €577. €686 + (0.5 × 577) = €974.5.

15. C is correct. Under the assumption of control, Zimt would record its own sales plus 100 percent of Oxbow's. €1,700 + 1,350 = €3,050.

16. C is correct. Net income is not affected by the accounting method used to account for active investments in other companies. "One-line consolidation" and consolidation result in the same impact on net income; it is the disclosure that differs.

17. B is correct. Statewide Medical was accounted for under the pooling of interest method, which causes all of Statewide's assets and liabilities to be reported at historical book value. The excess of assets over liabilities generally is lower using the historical book value method than using the fair value method (this latter method must be used under currently required acquisition accounting). It would have no effect on revenue.

18. A is correct. Under the equity method, BetterCare would record its interest in the joint venture's net profit as a single line item, but would show no line-by-line contribution to revenues or expenses.

19. C is correct. Net income will be the same under the equity method and proportional consolidation. However, sales, cost of sales, and expenses are different because under the equity method the net effect of sales, cost of sales, and expenses is reflected in a single line.

20. B is correct. Under the proportionate consolidation method, Supreme Healthcare's consolidated financial statements will include its 50 percent share of the joint venture's total assets.

21. C is correct. The choice of equity method or proportionate consolidation does not affect reported shareholders' equity.

22. A is correct. Revenue will not be higher for 2018 because Supreme Healthcare controls the SPE and thus eliminates intra-entity transactions and balances in consolidation. Consolidated revenue will thus present the results as if this transaction did not occur.

23. A is correct. Since the investment is designated as held-to-maturity, it is reported at amortized cost at 31 December 2016 using the effective interest method where the

amortization is calculated as the difference between the amount received and the interest income.

The interest payment each period is $500,000, which is calculated as the product of the par value of $10 million and the stated 5% coupon rate. The interest income of $440,000 is the product of the 4.0% market rate in effect when the bonds were purchased and the initial fair value of $11 million. The difference between the interest payment of $500,000 and the interest income of $440,000, equal to $60,000, is the amortization amount for 2016.

So, the initial fair value of $11 million is reduced by the amortization amount of $60,000, resulting in an amortized cost of $10.94 million at 31 December 2016.

24. B is correct. The SPE balance sheet will show accounts receivable of $50 million, long-term debt of $40 million, and equity of $10 million. When the balance sheets of Blanca and the SPE are consolidated, Blanca's cash will increase by $40 million due to the sale of the receivables to the SPE (net of its $10 million cash investment in the SPE). Long-term debt (non-current liabilities) will also increase by $40 million. So, the consolidated balance sheet will show total assets of $140 million and will look the same as if Blanca borrowed directly against the receivables.

Blanca Co. Current Balance Sheet (before consolidation)

Cash	20	Current liabilities	25
Accounts receivable	50	Noncurrent liabilities	30
Other assets	30	Shareholders' equity	45
Total assets	**100**	**Total liabilities and equity**	**100**

SPE Balance Sheet ($ Millions)

		Long-term debt	$40
Accounts receivable	$50	Equity	$10
Total assets	**$50**	**Total liabilities and equity**	**$50**

Blanca Co. Consolidated Balance Sheet ($ Millions)

Cash	$60	Current liabilities	$25
Accounts receivable	$50	Noncurrent liabilities	$70
Other assets	$30	Shareholder's equity	$45
Total assets	**$140**	**Total liabilities and equity**	**$140**

25. B is correct. The goodwill in Topmaker's $300 million purchase of Rainer's common shares using the equity method is $60 million, calculated as:

	$ Millions
Purchase price	$300
Less: 15% of book value of Rainer: (15% × $1,340)	201
Excess purchase price	99
Attributable to net assets	39
Plant and equipment (15% × ($3,160 − $2,900))	
Goodwill (residual)	60
	99

26. A is correct. Topmaker's representation on the Rainer board of directors and participation in Rainer's policymaking process indicate significant influence. Significant influence is generally assumed when the percentage of ownership interest is between 20% and 50%. Topmaker's representation on the board of directors and participation in the policymaking process, however, demonstrate significant influence despite its 15% equity interest.

27. B is correct. The carrying value of Topmaker's investment in Rainer using the equity method is $317 million and is calculated as:

	$ Millions
Purchase price	$300
Plus: Topmaker's share of Rainer's net income (15% × $360)	54
Less: Dividends received (15% × $220)	33
Less: Amortization of excess purchase price attributable to plant and equipment (15% × ($3,160 − $2,900)) / 10 years	3.9
Investment in associate (Rainer) at the end of 2016	$317.1

28. B is correct. The goodwill impairment loss under IFRS is $300 million, calculated as the difference between the recoverable amount of a cash-generating unit and the carrying value of the cash-generating unit. Topmaker's recoverable amount of the cash-generating unit is $14,900 million, which is less than the carrying value of the cash-generating unit of $15,200 million. This results in an impairment loss of $300 million ($14,900 − $15,200).

29. A is correct. According to IFRS, under the partial goodwill method, the value of the minority interest is equal to the non-controlling interest's proportionate share of the subsidiary's identifiable net assets. Rainer's proportionate share is 20% and the value of its identifiable assets on the acquisition date is $1.5 billion. The value of the minority interest is $300 million (20% x $1.5 billion).

30. A is correct. The current ratio using the equity method of accounting is Current assets/ Current liabilities = £250/£110 = 2.27. Using consolidation (either full or partial

goodwill), the current ratio = £390/£200 = 1.95. Therefore, the current ratio is highest using the equity method.

31. A is correct. Using the equity method, long-term debt to equity = £600/£1,430 = 0.42. Using the consolidation method, long-term debt to equity = long-term debt/equity = £1,000/£1,750 = 0.57. Equity includes the £320 noncontrolling interest under either consolidation. It does not matter if the full or partial goodwill method is used since there is no goodwill.

32. C is correct. The projected depreciation and amortization expense will include NinMount's reported depreciation and amortization (£102), Boswell's reported depreciation and amortization (£92), and amortization of Boswell's licenses (£10 million). The licenses have a fair value of £60 million. £320 purchase price indicates a fair value of £640 for the net assets of Boswell. The net book (fair) value of the recorded assets is £580. The previously unrecorded licenses have a fair value of £60 million. The licenses have a remaining life of six years; the amortization adjustment for 2018 will be £10 million. Therefore, Projected depreciation and amortization = £102 + £92 + £10 = £204 million.

33. A is correct. Net income is the same using any of the methods, but under the equity method, net sales are only £950; Boswell's sales are not included in the net sales figure. Therefore, net profit margin is highest using the equity method.

34. A is correct. Net income is the same using any of the choices. Beginning equity under the equity method is £1,430. Under either of the consolidations, beginning equity is £1,750 since it includes the £320 noncontrolling interest. Return on beginning equity is highest under the equity method.

35. A is correct. Using the equity method, Total asset turnover = Net sales/Beginning total assets = £950/£2,140 = 0.444. Total asset turnover on beginning assets using consolidation = £1,460/£2,950 = 0.495. Under consolidation, Assets = £2,140 – 320 + 1,070 + 60 = £2,950. Therefore, total asset turnover is lowest using the equity method.

 **CFA Institute**

ABOUT THE
CFA PROGRAM

The Chartered Financial Analyst® designation (CFA®) is a globally recognized standard of excellence for measuring the competence and integrity of investment professionals. To earn the CFA charter, candidates must successfully pass through the CFA Program, a global graduate-level self-study program that combines a broad curriculum with professional conduct requirements as preparation for a wide range of investment specialties.

Anchored by a practice-based curriculum, the CFA Program is focused on the knowledge identified by professionals as essential to the investment decision-making process. This body of knowledge maintains current relevance through a regular, extensive survey of practicing CFA charterholders across the globe. The curriculum covers 10 general topic areas, ranging from equity and fixed-income analysis to portfolio management to corporate finance, all with a heavy emphasis on the application of ethics in professional practice. Known for its rigor and breadth, the CFA Program curriculum highlights principles common to every market so that professionals who earn the CFA designation have a thoroughly global investment perspective and a profound understanding of the global marketplace.

www.cfainstitute.org

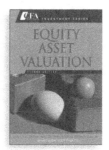

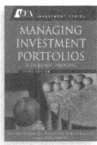

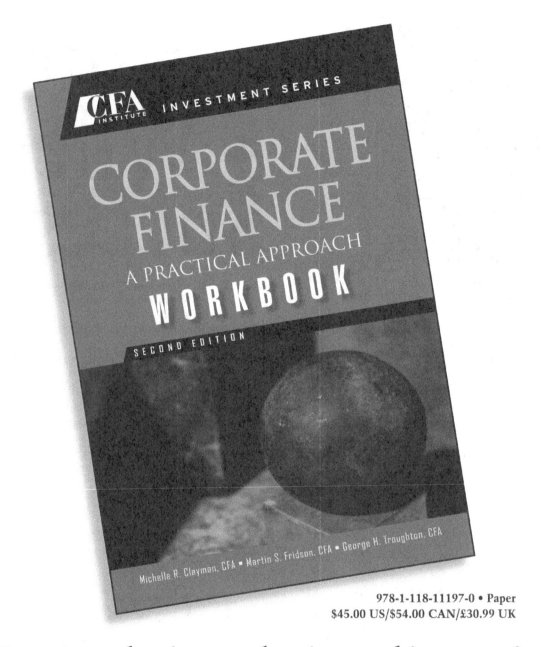